THE PARENT CONNECTION
AN EDUCATOR'S GUIDE TO FAMILY ENGAGEMENT

By Dr. Joni Samples

ENGAGE! PRESS 2009

The Parent Connection: An Educator's Guide to Family Engagment

ENGAGE! Press
411 N. Main Street
Galax, VA 24333

This book contains information gathered from many sources. The printer, publisher, and author disclaim any personal liability, either directly or indirectly, for advice or information presented within. Although the author, publisher, and printer have used care and diligence in the presentation, and made every effort to ensure the accuracy and completeness of the information contained in this book, we assume no responsibility for errors, inaccuracies, omissions, or any inconsistency herein.

First Printing 2009
ISBN No. 978–0–9814543–2–0
Library of Congress Cataloging–in–Publication Data

I dedicate this book to my kids,
Christopher, James, Jennifer, and Carolyn.

Thank-you for continuing to teach me everything I know about
parenting and learning.

ACKNOWLEDGMENTS

Ask and it is given. I asked and many people showed up to help me through the process of putting life to *The Parent Connection.*

My sincere thank-you goes to my writing teacher and mentor, Nora Profit, my wonderful editor, Vie Herlocker, and my book designer, Larry Van Hoose. Without these three people, I'd still be looking at scraps of paper covered with great ideas and no cohesion.

My deepest thanks to my four children, Christopher, James, Jennifer, and Carolyn, who allowed me to write articles about them from the time they were little and learning to be the wonderful adults they are today. I couldn't have done this without their love and support. I only heard an occasional, "Aw, Mom, did you have to tell that story?"

Thank-you to Sam Bartlett, who called me while I was writing this book and asked if I would consider bringing it to Family Friendly Schools and Engage Press for publication. The answer was yes, Sam. Thank-you for the opportunity to share *The Parent Connection* with you and so many others.

With gratitude, I want to thank my friends Reverend Duchess Dale and Don Converse. You have never asked me to be anything other than myself, or to give up my enthusiasm for what I love to do, even if it meant four o'clock a.m. emails, long walks around the lake, or missing dinner.

Thanks to my wonderful readers Nora, Vie, Sam, Don, Karen Hackett Villalobos, Elizabeth Morgan, and Ann Lambert. Each of you is very special and I appreciate you.

And last, my thanks to the wonderful administrators, teachers, support staff, parents, children, and all the rest who are so dedicated to helping children learn. I love the profession of teaching because it never lets you stop growing and becoming the best person you can possibly be.

Contents

Introduction

Years ago I taught third grade. The early months of the year were such a joy to teach. The children still loved their teachers and thought they knew everything in the world. The lessons hadn't gotten so hard that they lost confidence in their abilities, and life looked good from the playground view.

By the middle of the year, I saw some children beginning to struggle. The reading was getting harder, the spelling words longer, the math problems more complicated, and the content in the science book more complex. As learners, the children were falling into groups of those who were able to keep up with the increased demands and those who were not. I worried for those who were not making it. If they missed out now they'd miss out in every grade hereafter.

One evening at home, I had the idea that teaching parents how to help their children become more successful in school would help those in my classroom. Little did I know the actions I took would become a lifelong adventure into parent-teacher connections based on parents learning how to support their children's classroom instruction.

I taught a "help your child with reading" class for parents at the community college. I thought I knew what the parents needed to know, but the parents taught me what they wanted to know. They were my teachers. They taught me how to reach them, teach them, and support them while they taught their children.

I often remember those first sessions at the college, when my expectations and the parents' desires didn't always match. I became the student, who learned how to approach parents through their wants. And, every parent I've ever met or worked with wants his or her child to be successful.

Teachers have much the same goal. They want the students in their classrooms to be successful learners. My job and now yours, since you've decided to take on this very possible mission, is to help both parents and teachers facilitate success for children.

The Parent Connection is about helping you connect parents and teachers in the real world and work of raising successful children. For the purposes of this book, the reference to parents includes all other caregivers — extended family, foster parents, and other significant adults in the child's life. But how do we connect with each other? How do we make learning happen for children? How do we make learning fun, joyful, and meaningful?

Throughout this book, we will explore how our parent-teacher connections lead to school success. From the beginning stages of our own attitudes about each other, we'll move to building skills around a series of situations that lead to more and more collaboration and culminate in a plan for increasing learning.

Ultimately we will evaluate how our plan is going and tweak it as we go until we can say with surety and confidence, "Learning for our kids is going great!"

CHAPTER I

MAKING THE CONNECTION

Blayton School teemed with children inside its fences on a cool March day. I had been there before, but that was the first time I noticed the gates locked. Padlocks even secured the teachers' and visitors' parking lot behind eight-foot fences. I'd parked my car two blocks away and walked through the blustery wind to find monitors at the fences with fistfuls of keys. A supervisor motioned me around to the front where I found an open pass-through to get me to the office.

"Oh, it's you," mumbled the secretary, barely glancing up from the work on her desk. "You're in room 34. I think the janitor's down there. Come back and let me know if you can't get in and I'll page him."

Out of the eight hundred families in the school, only five parents arrived for the afternoon workshop.

A few days later in another part of the state, I pulled my car into the parking lot of Sun Empire School, a K-4 school of about four hundred children. March still wasn't over and the wind blew through the parking lot and on the playground there too. Children heading for buses, teachers chatting as they watched, and parents picking up the car-riders, all greeted me as I walked to the front door.

"Hi Dr. Joni," said the secretary as I entered the office. "Becky's expecting you. She's on the phone, but she'll be with you in a minute. Can I get you coffee or water? Everyone's looking forward to your workshop tonight. We're expecting over one hundred parents."

A Welcoming Environment

The choice is yours; do you want your school to be cold and unapproachable, or warm and welcoming? As an educational leader you take responsibility to make sure everyone feels wanted and valued. It's a big job, but someone gets the assignment, and most likely, you are the one.

When children and teachers feel comfortable in a school setting, they perform better. Teachers are more productive when they don't have a great deal of stress going on. Children achieve more when they're not worried about where dinner will come from or if their parents will be home when they get there.

Parents are the same way. When they feel positive, encouraged, and supported, they are more willing to collaborate with the school in their children's education. And, when parents engage with the school, everyone benefits, especially the kids.

Let's take a walk around a typical school. When you walk into the office, the place is probably buzzing with activity. The staff know what they're doing and seem to enjoy doing it. There's a bit of teasing going on and there's a big Happy Birthday sign on the wall for someone. Black balloons give a clue about the honoree.

As you walk down the hall, you meet several students. They smile and say hello before ducking into classroom doors. A teacher stops to ask a question. You enter the library and breathe in the smell of bindings and furniture polish. It's quiet except for the voice of a storyteller. Thirty children sit in front of her chair as she reads *Horton Hears a Who*. Their eyes never leave her or the book in her hand. Each child is anticipating the next picture to see if it matches with the one the words are creating.

Moving back into the hall, you see children tumbling out of classrooms headed for the cafeteria. A quick lunch and they'll be on the playground in ten minutes, burning off some of the physical energy they've been holding in most of the day.

Dropping by a couple of empty classrooms, you notice colorful bulletin boards, assignments on the chalkboards, books on desks, and projects that give you an overall sense of the place.

Similar classrooms, cafeterias, and curricula exist in schools around the world. But if schools were the same in every location, then every child would be learning and achieving like every other child in every other school. So why aren't they? The difference may be as simple as what we'll call your school's *well-being quotient*. How does your school feel? How does it feel to you? To your teachers? To the kids? To the parents? To the community? Is it a cold winter wind or a warm breeze? It's up to the educational leaders to keep the thermostat at the right temperature.

Motivation Keeps the Thermostat Up

Motivated kids mean learning is happening. Excitement and curiosity bring kids to school. They want to know what happened with Horton and Whoville. They want to see if the beans they planted came up. They want to count the number of stars they have on the bulletin board today. They want to see what their teacher has in store for them this week. You want students to come to school because they are attracted to what you do and what you teach. The school provides the catalyst by designing curriculum that is engaging and enjoyable. The kids provide the curiosity to see what happens next. When those pieces are working together, learning happens. When you walk through your school, does it feel like a place that you'd want to come to learn? Is it warm and inviting or an icy blast keeping even the hardiest at bay?

Tests and grades help to show how much progress you're making with instruction. A grade of *A* or *B* indicates student mastery of the material presented and tells educators they are on target. When grades of *D* and *F* occur, they reflect more than failure on the students' part. Poor grades show educators are not engaging or motivating children in ways that allow them to comprehend the information presented. Use standardized test scores and grades to analyze and modify what you're doing to re-engage a child in the classroom.

Tommy's Story

Tommy's second grade report card read like an evaluation for an employee about to be fired: Poor, Unsatisfactory, and Needs Improvement. It's not easy to do that at age seven, but he managed.

He didn't get reading. He could recognize a few words, but the concept of phonetically sounding out one letter then another took too long. He quit half way through. It wasn't a matter of vocabulary. His discussions about his interests in art and music convinced his teacher he had ability, but he couldn't read. After going through the eligibility process, Tommy qualified for special education.

The special education teacher provided interesting reading material at his level and supported him when he struggled. Tommy's breakthrough came one day when he was in the multipurpose room working on a computer. He was typing away when another child asked him what he was writing. *Eoseifmerolsd* wasn't a word Tommy could decipher.

Tommy hit the classroom in a temper matching his red hair. "I'm going to knock everything off this desk if you don't talk to me right now."

The teacher asked why he was so upset. Anger subsided to a flood of tears as Tommy told what had happened. Then he said, "I can't read. I want to learn to read."

Two years later, Tommy sat proudly with a group of gifted and talented students, his artwork receiving accolades and his math scores at the top of the class. Reading, although not perfect, had improved to grade level and Tommy walked with confidence into his regular education classroom.

Tommy's grades improved along with his self-esteem. His attendance improved and the redheaded troublemaker of the second grade no longer haunted the hallways of the school. An excited, motivated, fourth-grader showed up for school with the skills to do what was asked of him.

Students like Tommy exist in every one of our school systems. Whole schools are considered underachieving because the students who go there aren't learning what the state requires and the local board has adopted.

Referrals to the office for behavior often indicate children act out because they're not engaged in what is being taught. Attendance records show us children are absent more when the work is too hard or when they are "bored." Whenever you hear that word from children, they are saying the work is not motivating. Poor grades, below average test scores, and referrals are clues to how children respond to what we are trying to teach.

So What about the Other Excuses?

We recognize the difficulties some children experience. Poverty, home life, or families who speak a foreign language affect their worlds. All of that is understandable and very familiar in so many of our schools. We are caught in the excuses of poverty and the rest. The difficulties seem overwhelming for the students and for us. They are too big to change and too big to fight.

Yet, there is Tommy who, at eight, didn't want to be "excused." And there's Maria, a mom of three, who came to this country where she was denied recognition for all of her studies in Mexico. She had to start over, working two and three jobs, going to school, and raising her children. But she did not buy into any excuse. Today she proudly shares her story of getting her Associate of Arts degree saying she wants her children to have the education she had to work so hard to achieve.

There are children and parents out there who are willing to take this on with you. They are not willing to buy into excuses and situations. They are ready to join you in a battle to provide a quality education. This is your chance to work together with them to make it happen. This is your chance to make your school one that brings all players to the table and creates an atmosphere for learning that makes the difference you've been looking for.

Collaborating with Parents to Make a Difference

Every educator wants to leave a mark. Perhaps that is why you became an educator — to make a difference in a child's life. You want to know your life has an impact on others and you realize the children in your school are your legacy. As an administrator, teacher, or any part of a school, you continue to celebrate students' successes and feel their frustrations when they fail. You believe in them and you won't give up on them even when they give up on themselves.

You answered the call not only to become an educator, but also to become an educational leader. Each child who shows you a math paper, reads you a story, or gives you an art project is a symbol of your success. You are most satisfied when you are in an environment where children are learning under the care of nurturing and effective teachers. But, there are other adults in the lives of your students, — their parents or other caregivers — whose concern and love for each child exceeds that of even the most dedicated educators.

Suppose the people who care most about the children — the school administrators, teachers, support staff, and parents — could work together with a common set of goals for educational success? *It all begins when you invite the parents to join you in their children's learning experience.*

A look at the research shows why a positive approach to parent involvement improves our chances of attaining the results we want for kids and families. Anne Henderson, Senior Fellow at the Annenberg Institute for School Reform has been studying the effects of engaging parents in learning for over 25 years. In a report to the U.S. Senate Committee on Health, Education, Labor, and Pensions regarding NCLB reauthorization, she states:

> *When families are involved at home and at school, children do better in school, and the grades get better. The effects are greatest for low-income parents.*
>
> *In my most recent review of the research, which was written with Karen L. Mapp of the Harvard Graduate School of Education, and published by the Southwest Educational Development Laboratory in 2002, we found that students with involved parents, no matter what their income or background, are more likely to:*
>
> - *Earn higher grades and test scores, and enroll in higher-level programs,*
>
> - *Be promoted, pass their classes and earn credits,*
>
> - *Attend school regularly,*
>
> - *Have better social skills, show improved behavior and adapt well to school, and*
>
> - *Graduate and go on to post-secondary education. (Henderson, 2007)*

If the inclusion and training of parents bring about those results we'd be remiss not to explore the options. **It's time to build a relationship bridge between school and parents — it's time to make the parent connection.**

Ending the Mess We're In

Student performance and teacher accountability are visible in the media. The public holds administrators and teachers accountable for every child who loses a pencil, lies, or goes to jail. They scrutinize schools whose Adequate Yearly Progress (AYP) is below average and blame the educational system when students fail even outside of school. The schools didn't make the grade so the kids didn't either. Increasing motivation becomes difficult when the community and staff believe there's no hope of success.

Yet the research clearly shows performance can be improved. For most educational leaders, the question is how? How do I change performance when I'm barely hanging on with all the work I have to do now?

In the book, *The Presence Process: A Healing Journey into Present Moment Awareness*, author Michael Brown (2005) uses the term "mess-enders." He says messengers who get our attention are mess-enders. Poor academic performance, out-of-control behavior, or lack of successful programs may seem overwhelming, but they may actually be an opportunity to end the mess. Headlines in the newspaper about poor test scores in your school get your attention. Kids caught vandalizing the school get your attention. Loss of funds demands your attention. You need to deal with the mess as it arises, but this time let's see if there's a message in the mess that could be dealt with, resolved, and actually used to create a different way of doing business that will keep the mess from reoccurring.

There are people you might ask to assist in your mess-ending quest. These people are especially compelled to assist the students because they are their parents. And, no matter what their situation, they want their children to do well.

Elio Gonzales, a parent in a district in Central California, said it best during a parent workshop, "I work sixteen hours a day at two jobs. I've never attended school a day in my life. I don't want my children to have to work like I do. I want them to have an education and a better life."

Elio loves his four children. His eyes light up when he describes his eldest child's first days in college. From the reverence in his voice, the word *college* sounds like a cathedral. Elio is realizing his dream. His children believe in the life their father believes in. They want what he wants for them. And why not? Their bond is strong. They trust his judgment, and if education is his desire then they will be educated.

Parent /child bonding is evident in Elio's home as well as in the homes of gang members living down the street. Other parents may not have the same goals for their children as Elio. They may see money, drugs, or crime as a path to a better way of life. However, their children love them as Elio's children love him.

So when you ask these folks to help end a mess, you're taking a risk. It's a bit like asking someone to drive an eighteen-wheeler because he or she knows how to ride a bicycle. Yes, some parents have extremely interesting past and current lives. True some parents can't read or write themselves. Some don't have even the basic parenting skills to feed or clothe their kids.

But, if they learned how to ride a bicycle then they can learn how to drive a car and they can learn how to drive an eighteen-wheeler. If they want to learn and someone is willing to show them how, they'll learn. Elio had never been to school, but he is actively engaged in helping his children learn. That's possible, because someone took the time and resources to show Elio ways to help.

Educating parents, giving them the skills they need, and supporting them through their learning can make a difference for both the parent and the child in your school. Research proves it, teachers see it on tests and classroom performance, parents feel it, and kids know it.

Success Stories

You may still be a bit hesitant. It sounds like a good idea to include parents in the learning process, but it means changing your thinking. Does it make a difference if you connect with the parents or not? On the following pages, I'd like to share stories from a few schools that have found ways to include parents and experienced success as a result.

Live Oak Unified School District, a rural district in Northern California, had a vision of parents making a difference in their children's education. The community is diverse. Parents, who speak English, Spanish, and Punjabi, bring a mix of cultural influences along with their language differences.

Live Oak Director of Curriculum Meschelle Righero wrote her NCLB required plan for parent involvement then sought a way to implement it. She created a parent liaison position using Title I funds, and went to work to make her schools more parent-friendly. She met with administrators and staff members and worked to change old thinking. She set up workshops to show parents how to help their children learn. She provided childcare and translators, and ended every session with a family-style dinner. One of her teachers, Nicki Lleneras, caught the enthusiasm and demonstrated fun, easy activities for parents in both English and Spanish at every workshop.

Righero says, "You can feel the difference at the schools. The parents are taking an interest and they're doing learning activities at home."

In Phoenix, Arizona, the Murphy School District is also making a difference. Art Carrillo, a teacher-turned-administrator for parent and community engagement, didn't know exactly how to do the job he was assigned. He determined existing needs, and then he helped set-up food and clothing banks at each school and a medical clinic at one site. In the predominately Spanish speaking, inner-city schools, his Family Resource Centers organized bilingual classes to help parents strengthen their English, reading, and writing skills, and to show them how to help their children with the same skills. Parents now sit on district committees to design programs to help their children. The pride in the district and its children is evident when you go from school to school or speak to parents and staff members.

Sharon Carlton worked as an aide in the Marion County,

Tennessee, schools for several years before Title I funds put her in charge of technology and parent involvement. It wasn't long before Sharon built a team of Family Engagement Coordinators, the title given to a teacher from each site, which planned and coordinated family activities for the school. Carlton developed a training notebook and series of workshops to show each coordinator how to implement and track activities.

The program brought-in families from preschool to high school, and matched the needs of each school. Carlton maintains the project by providing on-going support and new ideas. She also shares her knowledge and experience with other Title I personnel.

Manuel J. Cortez Elementary School is in the country's fourth largest school district, Clark County, Nevada. Cortez had one of the lowest test scores in the district before they started a process of engaging their parents in education. Apartments and trailers surround the school, which is not far from the casinos and nightlife of downtown Las Vegas. Of the one thousand students, 99.7 percent are on free or reduced lunch. Yet a walk-though of this school showed why test scores had increased and morale was up. The teachers loved working there and said so; the children were engaged in their lessons, and had a variety of ways to learn; and the parents couldn't wait to show you "their space." A trailer in the parking lot housed a program where the parents could learn to read to their preschoolers, and where they learned about the curriculum in their older children's classrooms.

Paula Sutherland, an administrator from Bellevue School in Santa Rosa, California, explains her approach to their non-English speaking population. The school staff asked parents what they needed from the school. The answer was to learn English, so they could help their children learn. To address childcare needs, the school changed their early childhood after-school program schedules to coincide with the adult education program times. The adult education program used learning themes similar to the classroom lessons to help the parents learn English, which empowered them to assist their children with homework. The program was successful in bringing parents out, and Sutherland says, "Don't try to find a parking place around here on Monday through Thursday — there aren't any!"

Attitudes and academic programs change when schools and parents work together to provide what they need to support children.

When Parents Know They Can Count on You

Persuading yourself, then staff, and then parents often means a great deal of patience, support, and compassion. Be patient with yourself first. This may be a new adventure. You didn't learn to ride the bike overnight much less climb into the cab of the eighteen-wheeler and drive it down the freeway. Build your own understanding of what this means for you. You will need understanding to help both staff and parents to move through the process. Read, think, process, feel, and try out the concepts in this book. Allow the process to work for you. Let the changes come and be willing to dust yourself off and come back for more.

Enhance your credibility by your willingness to learn. Your parents can teach you as much as you teach them. They must rely on your trustworthiness to share their children, their concerns, and their point of view. When parents know they can count on you, they will inevitably be more trustworthy in return.

Graduation may be your ultimate goal for the kids in your school. Parents have the same goal, but the cap, gown, and graduation ceremony only represent the underlying desire for success that you and the parents have for their children.

Dr. Joni says…

- √ Excuses are just that.
- √ Connecting with parents begins with meeting their needs.
- √ Grades improve when parents are involved at home and at school.

CHAPTER II

P-TAG
YOUR SCHOOL'S PARENT-TEACHER
A TO G SUPPORT SYSTEM

Paper snowflakes dotted the windows of my daughter's third grade classroom. I'd left twenty telephone messages and rearranged three meetings to attend the play and luncheon that Carolyn and her classmates had been preparing for weeks. She'd asked me three times that morning if I was going to come and I assured her I'd be there.

Two children greeted me at the classroom door and invited me to sit wherever I wanted. Other parents were already filling the desks, so I joined a group of children standing to the side, awaiting their parts in the play. Soon, "reindeer" sporting red paper noses performed their lines and sang.

After the play, parents toured the room while the children readied lunch. The children around me scattered to help as my daughter showed me her desk, chair, books, papers, scissors, crayons, and paperclips.

Carolyn and I filled our plates at the luncheon table, and then we sat with the group of children I'd met earlier. We chatted about school, the play, and their teacher until all but one child went for seconds.

He and I talked for a minute, and then he looked at me and said, "My mommy would have been here today…" He hesitated, and then went on, "but she couldn't." The tears in his voice said it all.

I've held almost every role in education except driving a school bus. Yet in that child's simple words, I realized the importance of parents engaging in their children's education. That revelation added fuel to my personal journey to explore and strengthen the bond between parents and the schools. My daughter is grown with a child of her own now, but the lesson I learned in that third grade classroom became a stone in the foundation for P-TAG, a system I developed to help schools engage parents in learning.

So What is P-TAG?

P-TAG stands for Parent-Teacher A to G, a system that encourages parents and teachers to collaborate in educating the children. The letters A through G represent the process of building the relationship and moving forward with the goal of creating a successful learning experience for every child. A graphic representation and an overview of the system are included here. We'll go into more details and ways to implement this process in your school in later chapters.

In Step A of P-TAG, "Assess Attitude," you will assess the existing attitudes of staff and parents. You may be surprised to discover that not all staff or parents hold positive attitudes about the other.

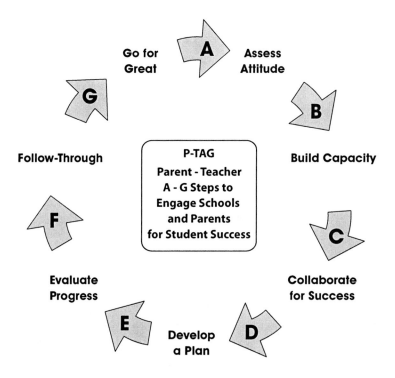

Attitudes change as relationships are established — but you must lead the effort by modeling and expecting a positive attitude from others.

Step B is "Build Capacity." This means you will start from wherever the parents are in their skill level and provide training in the skills they need. You will build the parents' capacity to support their children's learning. You will also build capacity in your staff to work with parents in educating their children.

In Step C, "Collaborate for Success," you will consider the importance of teamwork, and you will learn how to build the trust needed for a strong partnership between the school and the parents. You'll start with simple collaborative projects and create parent-teacher relationships that reflect mutual respect.

In Step D, you will "Develop a Plan" for your next collaborative project — one that directly meets children's learning needs. Your plan will be unique to your school and the team that creates it. It will reflect what your group sees as important and is ready to undertake.

Step E is "Evaluate Progress." Evaluation is part of any program we run in our schools. Educators collect data, analyze it, and decide which steps to take next. As you work through P-TAG, you will constantly evaluate results and adjust your plan to meet the needs.

Step F is "Follow-Through." Even with the best-developed plan and evaluation, you will need a system to ensure follow-through. New initiatives can easily slip in priority among the daily demands of working in a school. Follow-through keeps your plan on target for success. Follow-though also relates to the parents' commitment to be an active part of their children's education.

Step G, "Go for Great," is the wrap-up stage for P-TAG. You've worked through the steps, but as the schematic shows, P-TAG is cyclical and the steps are constantly in motion as your school moves towards excellence. When parents and teachers collaborate, when families are engaged in the learning experience, and when every student experiences success, then you "Go for Great!"

Getting Started on the Parent-Teacher Connection

Any project starts where you are right now. If you want to lose weight, you weigh yourself, set a goal, stop eating pizza and ice cream for six months, and weigh yourself again. You assess where you are at the beginning of the process, decide what you want the outcome to be, and then you work toward the goal you've set. Before you begin a parent-connection process at your school, let's weigh-in and gather baseline data.

Every school has data, sometimes more data than can humanly be absorbed. There are grades — grades on tests, grades on homework, grades on papers, and grades on report cards. Then there are state assessment tests — given annually and carrying so much weight that there are state and federal sanctions for poor performance. Furthermore, there are reports — attendance reports, budget reports, and newspaper reports shouting gang problems, poverty, or lack of school performance.

There's so much data that it's overwhelming at times. If you are dieting, all you want to know is how much you weigh and what to do about it. With so much information to choose from it's no wonder people throw up their hands and go have an ice cream cone. In our school's case, it's no wonder teachers go into their classrooms, shut their doors, and teach what they want to teach regardless of data, laws, and requirements. There's too much to deal with.

But you want children like my daughter and her little friend to have the best possible learning experiences, so you're willing to plow through the data to see what to do next. That's your headwork. Your heart work is the walk you took around the school to hear the Horton story and to watch the holiday play. You know how the school feels. How it feels — the school's well-being — is data too. All that information from both your head and your heart goes into making up the school that the children, the staff, and the parents know and sense every day of the week.

So you've gotten on the scale. You've done the baseline assessment necessary to see where your school is right now. If losing weight was the goal, you may be ready to change your eating habits and your exercise program. If improving your school's well-being and learning capacity is your goal, then you may need a different way of approaching the issues. The P-TAG system outlined in this chapter and delineated in the rest of this book, is a program for engaging your parents in their child's learning.

As with new eating habits and a new exercise program, you may have several desired outcomes — weight loss, better appearance, or improved health. With your P-TAG program, there can be a number of desired goals — improved test scores, enthusiastic students, fewer discipline problems, more parent support, increased staff morale, and the building of better community relationships. A successful diet requires that you stick to your good eating and exercise regime to reach your goals. When you stick to your P-TAG program, the result will be the same — you will see your parent-teacher connection goals come to fruition.

There are some basic guidelines to an eating and exercise plan, but you decide the specifics of how you'll carry it out. You choose when and what you will eat. You choose when, where, and how long you will exercise. You choose how fast you want to get to your goals. The same is true with P-TAG. The system provides the format for the A-G steps that work to get results. The P-TAG system allows choices that individualize the system for specific school goals. The choices are yours and the results are yours. You get to decide how best to include your parents, what projects you want to accomplish and whether, this year, you'll focus on improvement in reading or math.

P-TAG is for Everyone

Everyone is involved in the P-TAG system — administrators, teachers, support staff, parents, and children. Educating children requires all of us. Each of us does a different job to make the whole process work, and leaving one group out is like trying to drive a car with a flat tire. The car has difficulty rolling and eventually the tire shreds and the wheel becomes unusable. Ultimately, the car comes to a standstill. Standstills happen in your school when grades don't change, test results flatten out, and morale ebbs like the air leaking from a tire. When all areas are pumped-up, and the tires are checked often, the car keeps rolling.

Each person at your school has an important role, but all must be involved. The administrators make sure the school runs smoothly by taking care of the budget, handling academic and building issues, and providing overall leadership.

The teachers present the curriculum, motivate students, and encourage parent involvement. The support staff — secretaries, bus drivers, cafeteria workers, nurses, and custodians — provide the background threads in the school's tapestry. They bring the children to school, feed them, bandage them, and provide a clean environment for them.

The job of parents is to support their children's learning. Parents do this by ensuring their children are in school, expecting homework to be completed, and attending school functions. They also consult with the teachers on ways to reinforce skills from the classroom. The students have their jobs, too. We expect them to attend to instruction, complete their work, and take tests with integrity.

The roles may differ, but each player is an integral part of the whole of learning.

Few schools are currently rolling smoothly down the road with all players engaged. Mostly we find schools where a tire, or several tires, leak. In some places, the tire is flat and the vehicle is sitting on the roadside. The individuals in the school are on the side of the road waiting for a ride, a tow, or anything to get started again.

It's time to change the tire. It's time to refill it with a breath of fresh air, new life, and energy. Integrating each of the players into a cohesive team for making learning happen is the key to bringing back the joy and excitement of teaching.

Empowering Parents

The P-TAG system is simple. The steps focus on parent and teacher connection because parents work closer with their child's teacher than with anyone else in the school. Often, parents are the members of the team who are least included, but everyone benefits when parents are involved. Many parents are unaware of the things they can do to help their children. Yet, when the school shares strategies to support learning at home, the parents are eager to help.

Empowered parents feel more comfortable collaborating with the teachers, and their support for the entire school increases. When this happens, the school administrator's job gets easier. Teachers are energized because children are more engaged in learning. Bus drivers, noon-duty aides, and secretaries find the children quicker to listen and follow directions. The students are excited about learning because they know adults at school and at home care about what they are doing. This is what we call a win-win-win-win situation.

The A-G steps in the P-TAG program are straightforward and cyclical. You will do steps A, B, and C with your current crop of parents and then several new families will enroll their children in your school, or new kindergarteners will begin their school year. These new families will need to have a connection so they know the school cares about them. You'll need to cycle them through. In Step D, you'll develop a family learning plan, and in Step E, you'll evaluate it only to find modifications to the plan are necessary. In the meantime, you'll find parents and teachers are feeling good about what's happening at the school. The system cycles, so you won't be resting on one set of accomplishments. You'll be making many changes and that's good. It is the beginning of a big change.

The Biggest Change is a Change in Thinking

The P-TAG program is an investment in you, the rest of the school staff, and your community, it doesn't have to cost a lot of money, but it does require a change in thinking. You are looking at a large number of people — the families of your students — to provide additional support for learning. You may need to reallocate your current staffing, time, or funding, but the results are worth the effort. You, the rest of the staff, and the parents will determine what those reallocations look like.

Bellevue School's direction was to help parents learn English so they could support their children. A reallocation of services went into making that happen. The school already had all the programs in place: adult education, after school programs, and state preschool. They only needed to rearrange the programs to support their need. Their California test results showed an increase in student achievement and attainment of their growth target. Parent comments, posted on www.greatschools.com, reflected positive statements about both teachers and programs. Parents at Bellevue School, as in most schools, wanted more music and extracurricular activities, but they felt the regular academic programs were solid and supportive.

Team Support

Your P-TAG Support System will involve a team representing members of each of your groups — administrators, teachers, support staff and parents. Some schools use their existing leadership team. That's fine if all groups are represented on that team.

The flexibility of P-TAG allows you to customize your plan and your timetables for implementing it. You can meet with your team daily, weekly, or monthly to have your system start taking affect. It's up to you. However, it is important to meet consistently, follow the steps of the system, and keep track of where you are in the process in order for your team to see progress. Your team may suggest rearranging your current resources to support the intent of the team.

A sample checklist for the P-TAG process is included in the Appendix. This checklist will help you identify what support is necessary to assist staff, parents, and students through the P-TAG process. Some schools will need to start at the beginning of the system and take each step in order. Other schools have already done some of the preliminary work — they may have collected data, assessed attitudes, and already started building capacity. Those schools can skip Steps A and B and go to Step C or D. Most schools, however, will want to recycle through certain sections and come back to the section chapters to review, rewrite, and rejuvenate. All of the above are encouraged.

Are you ready? Let's get started!

Dr. Joni says...

√ There is no cost to changing your thinking!

√ No matter their age, students want their parents involved in their lives.

√ Empowered parents feel more comfortable collaborating with teachers, and their support for the whole school then increases.

CHAPTER III

A — ASSESSING ATTITUDE

Thoughts create emotions and over time, those emotions build attitudes. For example, follow this line of thinking: *These families live in poverty. They grew up in poverty. Their children live in poverty. They don't have anything. If they don't have anything, they can't give anything to their children. They can't teach them anything because they don't have anything. They're worthless. There's nothing you can do to help.* Soon that mantra becomes an attitude of odds too impossible to overcome. When those attitudes permeate a school, children, teachers, and parents feel it.

In Step A of P-TAG you will look at attitudes — yours, the rest of the school staff,'s and the parents'. You'll review attitudes and determine if you need to make adjustments before addressing major issues. It's not likely someone with a negative attitude will jump in to work on a new parent project. That person already *knows* the parents *can't* and *won't*. Negative attitudes are the death knell to your plan. The first step is to identify those attitudes and do what it takes to change them.

Attitudes change when there's evidence that substantiates a reason for change. P-TAG activities promote collaboration between parents and teachers and open new avenues of thinking. New avenues of thinking change old beliefs, and soon attitudes begin to shift.

Expect Positive Attitudes from Staff Members

Hamilton High School sits on Highway 32 between Orland and Chico, California, in a town of about nineteen hundred people. Ray Odom has walked the hallways of Hamilton High since he was a student there back in, well, who knows how long ago that was. He is now the Superintendent/Principal of Hamilton High School. Ray grew up with many of the families in Hamilton City, yet he still visits the home of every incoming freshman. He goes to ease the transition, answer questions, and show he values the student and family. Ray's visits may be the first connections parents have to the high school. You can be sure they are a bridge for future parent/school involvement.

That's not the only story about Ray's commitment to families. Here is what one teacher shared:

Ray makes a big deal of what is talked about in the teachers' lounge. Anything is fair game except talking negatively about students or their families. One afternoon, a teacher was verbally taking it out about a student and the student's family. You can imagine the comments, "Johnny/Juan/ Susie is such a pain. He/she can't ever get the work in, doesn't care, and is a major screw up. The family never comes to school for anything. They're no help at all. This kid is going to end up….." You can fill in the rest.

The teachers' lounge window was open and Ray happened to walk by. He did an about-face, opened the door, and asked the teacher to step into his office. The window to Ray's office wasn't open, but there was little doubt a conversation about attitudes of respect — and Hamilton High expectations — was taking place.

Ray's leadership contributed to Hamilton High receiving one of three California Distinguished School Awards. Part of the review process for the award included student interviews — and when students describe their school as the most supportive place in the community, you know you are doing things right. Ray believes in his students and his attitude permeates his staff's attitudes.

How's your attitude? Do you enjoy getting up in the morning and heading for your school? Or, do you drive by Wal-Mart wondering if they might need a new greeter? We all have days where being behind the perfume counter at Macy's looks a lot more enticing than another battle with the budget, the board, or the bus schedule, but overall, do you want to be in your school? If your answer is no, then look for the place you want to be and go enjoy it. Seriously, it's time for you to find what's right for you. You need to enjoy your life everyday, so match your skills with what you want to be doing. When you enjoy life more, so will your students.

Which One Are You?

Have you heard this story? A nomad wandering across the desert came to the gate of a town. He asked the wise man at the gate if the town was friendly and welcoming or hostile and cold. The wise man asked the nomad, "What was the town like where you came from?"

The nomad answered, "It was awful. The people were mean and cruel. They gossiped and no one helped each other. It was a horrible place."

The wise man said, "This town is the same as where you were before." The nomad didn't even enter the city. He went on his way.

Shortly another man entered the city. He also asked the wise man at the gate, "What is this town like?"

The wise man asked, "What was the town like where you came from?"

"Oh," answered the man, "it was wonderful. The people were warm and friendly. They'd go out of their way to help one another. I loved living there, but I had to move on for my work."

"Welcome," said the wise man. "This town is the same as where you were before." The man happily entered the gate.

What's your attitude as you enter the gates of your school? Is Macy's calling, or are you ready to join the warm, friendly group waiting inside? Your mindset permeates every action and decision you make. Attitude begins and ends with you.

Attitude Check-Up — Yours

Attitude deals with how you think and feel. You adjust your attitude by adjusting your thinking. If you think people around you are awful, stupid, or lazy and they don't get it, then your attitude may need a tune-up. We're talking about attitude here, not test scores or crunching budget numbers.

"Think positively and everything will be fine." That's easy to say, but look at this budget, look at the economy, or look at whatever else is bothering you. And if you only see the reasons why you can't achieve the school's full potential, then you won't move forward. Like attracts like. Thinking about what's not working will continue what's not working.

The trick is to imagine what your school can be, and give your full attention to that image, being sure your image will become reality. This is the art of deliberate creation.

Andrew Carnegie, Napoleon Hill, and more recently, Jack Canfield utilized the concept of deliberate creation for running businesses and amassing fortunes. The techniques work as well when creating a school that meets the expectations of "having it all." There are a number of books on positive thinking listed in the appendix and many more in the bookstores.

If you like being in education, see yourself as making a difference, and enjoy interacting with students, staff, and families at your school, then you'll continue to see and do more of the same. If you can imagine an even better vision for your students and families, then you will deliberately create that situation. Your thinking will propel you toward situations that will improve current conditions.

When you have a vision for your school, and your attitude is on-target, then it's time to look at the rest of the school.

Teachers at Heart

Teachers are the heart of a school. They keep the blood pumping and flowing into the lives of the children in their classrooms. The easiest place to access the attitudes of teachers is in the teachers' lounge. Have lunch in the lounge and listen. Are the comments positive and supportive toward kids? How about toward families? Could a new family in the neighborhood sit in the teachers' lounge and be comfortable? Would they bring their children back the next day or would they enroll their children in the school down the block?

Listen carefully. Identify teachers who consistently say the positive things about children and families. Associate yourself with those teachers because they're the ones who will encourage access to your school. Those teachers will build parent connections with you. You may need a Ray Odom intervention with some members of the staff, but it won't take long before the message is clear — we support children and families here.

Attitudes and Traditions Create Culture

The culture of a school consists of attitudes and traditions created and developed over years of practice. You felt it when you walked onto the school grounds. You noted it in the office at the front desk. You sensed it in the classrooms. It's there. The school's culture invites you in or turns you away. There's no judgment here about your culture. It is what it is. It's been growing for years, a bit like mold, in the walls, nooks, and crannies of your school facility as well as the hearts and minds of your staff and students.

If this is a good mold like that used in blue cheese dressing, keep it and grow more of it. If it's one you'd clean out of the back of your refrigerator (because you can no longer identify what it's growing on) then it's time to do some rethinking.

The mold didn't grow overnight. A once-fresh food, plan, or attitude grew old and rotten, and no one wanted to throw it out. It was easier to push it to the back of the refrigerator and pretend it wasn't there. There are moldy thoughts in your school. You know the ones: *The kids here are low income/don't speak English/can't learn anything/ and their families are not involved. There's not enough money/time/support to do our jobs. I am not paid to do any more than I'm doing.*

The list can go on, but you know the thoughts in your school. Get rid of those rancid attitudes today. Those thoughts drain the energy and joy out of teaching. It's time to try something fresh, healthy, and satisfying. To get rid of the mold growing in the back of our minds, we need to revise our thinking. We must believe the students who come to us are successes just as they are. We must believe the families who live in our neighborhoods want their children to do well and are willing to help them and to help us.

Head Office

If the heart of the school is found in the teachers' lounge, the head of the school is in the front office. That's the first place a new staff member goes. That's the first place a visiting parent goes. How's the attitude in your front office?

In *Engaging All Families*, Steve Constantino (2003), a former high school principal, tells about the first time he walked into the front office of his newly assigned school. There was a long front counter with a desk behind it. The secretary hardly looked up when he introduced himself as the new principal. She pointed to an office and said, "You're over there." By noon the next day, Steve had the custodians remove the front counter and move the secretary's desk. The new staff member sitting at the desk was to greet people as they came in and ask what she could do to help them. Didn't take long. What it takes is a change of attitude, or sometimes, a change of personnel.

When your front office isn't providing the positive attitude your school desires, change what you're doing. Rearrange the furniture, change the posters on the bulletin boards, repaint the walls — even small changes can make the front office a more family friendly place.

Office staff should answer phone calls in a friendly and inviting manner. Be sure the recording on your answering machine communicates a positive attitude, too. Call a few offices, any kind of office, and listen to the reception. Do you feel like the person on the other end of the phone is there to help you and wants to talk with you? Or do you feel more like you're talking to a computer? How long are you placed on hold? Call your office. Are you being helped or put on hold? Train or retrain the person answering the phone if necessary.

I had several phone interactions with one school, and no matter who answered, they were upbeat, positive, and took care of my needs. One day I told the receptionist how much I enjoyed talking to anyone in the office. She responded, "We're trained to do that. And we like it."

Look at the correspondence from your office. Does it look like a friendly reminder or an IRS tax form? If families don't come to school often, it may be because your correspondence carries an attitude of, "We're going to make everything so complex it will keep you away." Make your correspondence eye-catching, jargon-free, and in the language families prefer.

A respectful attitude from the front office goes a long way in creating an atmosphere that encourages both staff and parents to participate in learning.

Allocating Energy, Attention, and Time

Another measure of attitude is how you use your time. You wake up in the morning, have a cup of coffee, and begin planning for the day. Many of us have a list of priorities. I like to call those my intentions. Our intentions may be great, but we all know our day will be filled with interruptions — especially in a school.

As interruptions occur, we have to make decisions based on their urgency and importance. Some interruptions require immediate attention. In *Building Better Schools by Engaging Support Staff* (Bartlett and Herlocker, 2007, 77-80), these interruptions are called L.I.O.N.s, because Like It Or Not, they must be dealt with right away. Other interruptions may not be as pressing, but often we attend to them as if they were urgent. At the end of the day, we have not completed all of our priorities or intentions.

An example occurred while I was writing this section. I intended to write a chapter when I sat at the computer, but an email from a friend asking for assistance on a school discipline issue distracted me. I spent thirty minutes researching the information, finding the right contacts, and emailing an answer. By that time, I was off target with my original goals for the day. It took another fifteen minutes to refocus on what I wanted to accomplish. Overall, I'd lost about forty-five minutes of time and a lot of momentum.

We may do this to ourselves so many times during the school day we end up exhausted and wondering why we are not progressing toward our goals. How you allocate your energy, attention, and time is directly related to the attitude or the mind-set you have about your school. Set your priorities at the beginning of your day, and then allocate your resources to complete those activities that match your vision. Don't lose sight of those opportunities to connect with staff, parents, and students who hold the same vision — when you think about it, those moments represent the highest priority in an educator's day.

Open Invitation

What would make your school a more inviting place? Consider this example of a staff creating a positive learning environment.

Peabody Elementary is a three-story remodeled building squeezed into a residential area of Washington, D.C. In 1995, teachers in the school applied for and received permission to open a School-Within-A-School. They wanted to incorporate the techniques of Reggio Emilia, a hands-on discovery methodology for learning, in their preschool and kindergarten programs. The teachers obtained grants to enhance their program and to equip an art studio. When I visited, Peabody was buzzing with energy and excitement about learning. Their positive attitude began at the front door.

The principal and teachers at Peabody had such a positive attitude about their school I remember it years later. The staff at Peabody worked together to select the programs they wanted to put into practice. They attended in-services to learn how to implement the programs, and budgeted both time and resources to make it happen. Making your school memorable isn't as hard as it might seem. It all starts with attitude.

Attitudes toward Parents

Our focus for this book is the connection we make with parents. It's only logical we look at our attitudes toward the other adults surrounding the children we serve.

Live Oak is a school district with a central office administrator who includes staff and parents as partners in learning. A first, a third, and an eighth grade teacher joined the director around a conference table in the district office for a brainstorming session. Ideas flowed with the belief that engaging parents would enhance learning. The resulting plan included several parent workshops where parents would receive the *Parent Playbook* series (Samples, 2007) in their native language.

The teacher input varied at the meeting. One teacher eagerly selected activities from the *Playbook* to demonstrate at the parent workshop.

Another was reluctant to speak to a large group. She liked the concept of engaging parents, but did she have to talk to them?

The third teacher had his own plans. It was a good idea, but he was busy. How would this benefit him? Why not give the parents the books and let them do whatever they wanted? They could help or not, it was up to them.

All three teachers had legitimate concerns that directly affected their time and their focus. They talked. Communication and collaboration brought out a number of issues in their own lives as well as in the school.

These teachers had children of their own. Soon the discussion turned to how much they tried to support their own kids, but how life, job, and energy sometimes weren't up to the task. They acknowledged their education background helped them, and considered how parents without a similar level of training might find schoolwork a challenge. They shared how they each learned new skills, and admitted sometimes it took a person with different skills or training to demonstrate programming the latest electronic gadget or installing the sink — tasks they could do themselves, *after being shown how.*

By the end of the conversations, the first teacher was even more enthusiastic about demonstrating activities at a workshop and was figuring out how to get parent engagement activities home with her kids each week. The second teacher was sure she could do at least one activity for the parents, and she wanted to try out some of the literacy activities in her classroom. The third teacher was quiet for a minute, and then he said, "I get it. They need to see it done if they're going to try it at home. I'll be at the workshop and I get to go first to share an activity. They need to know how important it is they get involved."

Often times we resist something or someone new. Resistance

comes from not feeling comfortable. Adding parents to the school mix is definitely new, and educators are accustomed to working alone in their school silo. When questions are answered and a level of comfort created, the resistance diminishes or disappears. Involve teachers in order to involve parents. We'll talk more about specific ways for teachers and parents to build, collaborate, and plan in the next three chapters, but for now, take the time to adjust attitudes. The more positive the attitude and the clearer the vision of a collaborative parent-teacher effort for increased academic achievement, the more likely you will meet your goal.

Your Attitude Attracts More of the Same

Start with your attitude. Keep it positive and upbeat. When you feel it ebbing, take control of your thoughts, and turn them to the positives in the situation. Focusing on the negative will only get you more of the negative. Focus on what is working and expand those thoughts. Focus on the vision and propel yourself toward it. Elizabeth Scott (Ask.Com) says this about attitudes:

> *By focusing on attaining a new reality, and by believing it is possible, we tend to take more risks, notice more opportunities, and open ourselves up to new possibilities. Conversely, when we don't believe that something is in the realm of possibilities for us, we tend to let opportunities pass by unnoticed. When we believe we don't deserve good things, we behave in ways that sabotage our chances at happiness. By changing our self-talk and feelings about life, we reverse the negative patterns in our lives and create more positive, productive, and healthy ones. One good thing leads to another, and the direction of a life can shift from a downward spiral to an upward ascent.*

Strengthen your own positive attitude. Reinforce the positive attitudes of your staff. As a coach encourages the players on a team, you can also be a staff coach. To take on new challenges like a Reggio program or new partners like parents, you'll need confidence and a positive attitude. Give your staff the encouragement they need. Many schools have a "catch a child being good" program that recognizes students for acts of kindness, demonstrations of courtesy, and other positive behaviors. Expand the program to "catch a staff member being positive." Then expand it even further to "catch a parent being engaged in learning." Encourage, build, and grow positive attitudes every day of your school year.

Dr. Joni says…

√ Everything begins with attitude.
√ The attitude you display attracts more of the same.
√ Make your school positively memorable!

Chapter IV

B — Build Capacity

As educators, we go to school to learn subject matter like science or social studies. Then we learn how to teach the content we've learned. It's our job to be knowledgeable as well as to be able to impart knowledge to children.

Parents who choose to become engaged in school and learning activities are often stepping out of their comfort zones. They know how to clean house, make meals, go to work, and take the kids to baseball games, but it's intimidating to take on anything that looks like teaching. Parents didn't get a degree in parenting with an emphasis in helping their child learn to read.

Educators can help parents increase their skills and confidence to teach their children. This process is referred to as "building capacity," and it requires we start wherever the parents are in their skill level and give them specifically designed activities to develop the skills they need to help with their children's learning.

Building capacity is about showing parents how to do what we do. It's all about training and support. It's about helping the parents help themselves so they help their children. Start wherever the need is. Murphy School District started with the basics of food, clothing, and a medical clinic on school grounds. That's what was needed. You start where you are and build for more. It will take the whole team pulling together to identify where to start, and then what and how to build.

Combat Staff Reluctance

We could stop here and focus on what the parents need in order to be successful, but there is a piece the school staff needs too. Often there is reluctance on the part of school folks to include parents. Your staff may have thoughts like these: *Parents aren't capable of teaching, they aren't trained, they'll interfere with what we teach, they'll confuse the kids, and a whole lot more.*

The bottom line is fear. Parents are afraid to teach their children because they're not sure what to do. Educators are afraid to have parents teach the kids because they may not do it right. It's time we stop being afraid of what the other might or might not do and create a way for both parents and teachers to work together to support children's learning.

The parents in your school come with a myriad of skills. You have singers, performers, laundry workers, custodians, doctors, and farm hands.

John is a carpenter. He builds houses, lays floors, and creates space for people to live in. All day he measures, calculates angles, and adds up the costs of his materials. He paints rooms. He determines the space he has to cover, how much paint it will take, and what it will cost him in time and labor to paint the room. He has five children in your school.

Julie does part-time work as a bookkeeper. She keeps books for a dozen of the businesses around your school. She also does taxes for her neighbors and a few clients. She has two children in your school.

Carlos is a writer. He teaches writing and English as a Second Language classes for the community college in the evenings. He's published two books, several articles, and has his own blog. He has three children in your school.

John may not realize his five children could benefit from knowing how to measure, calculate angles, and figure cost. He takes his skills for granted and assumes his children will learn math in school. He may be surprised to find out one of his children is having a problem with basic addition and he could help. Julie and Carlos also have wonderful skills to share with their children

These parents and others have abilities and expertise to help their children, but they probably don't even realize it. Like most of us, they evaluate their skills in relationship to a job they perform. They may have confidence in their work and not even know those skills are the very ones their child is studying at school.

Our job is to help parents identify skills, build confidence, and show them how they can use their knowledge to help their children.

Focus on Abilities

Our thinking is often about what people can't do. You undergo a job assessment to show skill level in math and end up feeling frustrated because you can't do the geometry problems. You look at the advertisements for art schools and draw the bird in the test box. Then you never sign up for lessons because your beak looks like a pencil and the wing is bigger than the body. It is easy to give up and put both math and art into a box labeled, "Things I Can't and Won't Ever Be Able to Do."

Focusing on deficits or not being perfect means putting many things in that box. To engage parents at your school, you'll need to focus on their strengths and assets instead. Here are a few skills you might find:

√ John's ability to do geometry

√ Julie's ability to add, subtract and possibly take care of the cafeteria fund

√ Carlos's writing and tutoring skills

√ Jose's ability to fix a truck

√ Dr. Lynch's skills in showing a class how to do basic first aid

√ Jennifer's sign language

√ Maria's skills in translation

√ Dora's love for infants and toddlers (especially useful for school events)

Your school is ready to involve those who can support your educational goals. Consider the opportunities to use parents as you would any volunteers coming into your school. You can fill-in pages of skills, but you'll have to discover them first. Parents don't often show up to say I can translate or show children how to do first aid. If they did, you might not need a procedure in place that would allow them to share their skills. You'll need to do some groundwork to set up opportunities. Then you're going to find out who and what you have in your community.

Enhancing Your Program with Engaged Parents

Let's start by determining what you'd like parent engagement in your school to look like. Your vision must meet the individual needs of your school and community. The model you create will not be the same as the cross-town school's model. So, how can the parents' skill sets enhance your educational program? Do you need classroom assistants in the primary classrooms? Field trip chaperones? Technology support to set up your computer lab? Translators for other parents? Parents to create materials for the teachers? These are only a few of the parent engagement activities going on in schools right now. You can do any or all of the above. Engagement depends on what your school envisions it to be.

P-TAG takes the vision for engagement beyond parents assisting only within the building. Yes, it is important to have parents engaged in classroom and school-wide projects, but what about the ones who can't come in? P-TAG includes parents working with their children at home on learning activities. The goal is to have every family working nightly and on weekends to support school learning. When family learning is the goal, schools engage parents in the building as well as those who can't be there.

Now take a few minutes to close your eyes and imagine your

school — teachers, parents, students, support staff, building, all of it — as you want it to be. As you know it can be.

From Vision to Policy

Do you have a vision for your school? Good. Now let's create a policy that supports the vision. Sometimes our policies sound like a doctor's statement of what could go wrong with the operation he's about to perform. "You have a 95 percent survival rate with this appendectomy, but if something should go wrong you could die from fungus, peritonitis, abdominal trauma, or thirty-two other related problems."

If parents feel the policies are negative or so technical they can't understand them, they won't read past the first paragraph. Your policies should be clear and written in a family friendly style. Let's look at a sample policy:

> *The school wishes to include all members of a child's learning community in the learning process. Parents are encouraged to participate in all school functions, interact with their child's teacher, and help with learning both in and out of the classroom. We recommend a minimum of forty hours a year of participation in some type of school activity.*

Although participation cannot be required, it can be encouraged and when you include it in your vision and your policy, you will need to find ways to make it happen. Ask yourself how different your school would be if every parent gave forty hours of participation each year.

When you ask for commitment, be ready for parents who are willing to give you the hours you've asked for. The front desk is a good place to start. Make sure your receptionist/secretary responds positively to parent requests to help and has information available to share with the parent. The following items should be available in the front office:

- √ A volunteer contact form that includes name, address, e-mail address, phone number and what they are willing to do
- √ A list of current needs generated and regularly updated by staff members
- √ Materials available for parents who want to do activities at home
- √ A list of the legal requirements for working with the school

Make sure your legal requirements for volunteering in the building are clear. Have a system to make the requirements easy for the parents to meet. Do volunteers need a driver's license and insurance to go on a field trip? If they're working in the classrooms, do they need fingerprints or a background check? Arrange for the fingerprint technician to come to the school and process a group of parents during a volunteer meeting. Do whatever you can to remove obstacles to parent engagement in your school.

Designate a staff member to coordinate volunteer assignments within the building. Don't forget to have a volunteer sign-in sheet in the front office to document the time donated to the school.

Make sure your teachers can say, "Yes, I'd love to have you help with what we're doing in the classroom this year." Here is a checklist to help teachers answer when a parent asks if they can help:

- √ Check parents' name, address, and phone number with the emergency information on file. Get an e-mail address if one is available.

√ Have a list of volunteer opportunities in the classroom. These might include helping at a center, listening to children read, cutting out pieces for a bulletin board, going on a field trip, bringing snack,s etc.

√ Have a list of activities parents can do at home with their children, such as reading stories, playing math games, practicing spelling words, writing stories, and playing games. *The Parent Playbook* (Samples) series provide home activities matched to state learning standards. Many schools use this series to give parents a systematic and fun way to work with their children.

√ Keep track of parent involvement time and coordinate with the person assigned to track parent hours.

Parent Liaison Elizabeth Morgan took on the task of coordinating parent time and talent at St. Hope School in inner city, Sacramento, California. The following chart shows what happened at St. Hope when parents were requested to donate forty hours a year to the school.

Please note the increase in both parent involvement percentages and in testing scores. From 2006 to 2007, the scores increased fifty-three points on the state yearly assessments. Similar schools increased only fourteen points. That's significant by any school's standards.

Academic Results and Parent Involvement PS7's Results

	API Score	Involvement %
2003-2004	638	70%
2004-2005	737	88%
2005-2006	744	94%
2006-2007	749	*
2007-2008	802	98%

Academic Rigor + Parent Involvement = Student Achievement!!

Build Relationships to Build Capacity

In order to know your parents and the skills they possess, you'll need to meet them first. A middle school principal invites parents for coffee one morning each week. A parent liaison has Tuesday Tours, where she takes a group of parents to visit classrooms and chats about school functions and learning along the way. Ray Odom visits homes of new students, and Meschelle Righero meets parents at the workshops and family dinners in her district. Decide what works best for you and your community, but make it your goal to meet and know every family.

Magdalena was reluctant to come to school. She didn't speak English and had only completed fourth grade. She said she didn't feel right there. I kept asking. I kept connecting. She eventually showed up at a parent workshop, then a second. By the end of the series, she had attended every session for both her first grader and her fourth grader. At the end of each parent workshop, I always asked the parents to tell one thing they planned to do with their children during the next week. After a few weeks, reluctant Magdalena looked forward to sharing her ideas with the group.

If you have reluctant parents, keep asking and connecting. Offer your help if needed, and be sure to follow through. Be patient. Parents may be working through trust and confidence issues, so your commitment, patience, and perseverance are required.

A few years ago, I visited a large elementary school in San Antonio, Texas. I had an appointment with a vice-principal who was going to take me on a tour of their summer school program. She came out of her office to greet me, and then said, "Will you excuse me for a moment." She stepped around the counter to hug a Hispanic man and his wife. "We're so glad you're back," she said. "If there's anything we can do to help, we'll be there. There's a prayer group on Wednesday evening here. Please come. We'll all be looking for you."

After chatting for a minute more she stepped back to me and asked me into her office. As we walked in she said, "Juan recently got out of jail. We're so glad to see him back and his family is so glad he's home." That is knowing a family, and you must know your families before you can build their capacity to collaborate with the school in the education of their children. When the leadership of the school demonstrates that knowing and supporting families is a top priority, other staff members will notice.

If Juan had been a parent in your school, would the teachers' lounge talk be about the loser guy who can't get it right and is always in trouble, or would the conversation be how to help Juan and his family while he's readjusting to being home? Your respect of families is the model for the others in the school. The positive words you speak will encourage other staff members to do the same — and remember that building capacity depends on a respectful relationship.

Build Confidence to Build Capacity

A drawback for parent participation may not be unwillingness or lack of time. It may be lack of confidence. John may not think he reads well so he doesn't show up at school to help. School is where you read. Julie may think bookkeeping isn't really math. It's adding and subtracting, not algebra or anything important. Carlos is busy and doesn't see how what he does could fit in anywhere.

An example of lack of confidence arose in a parent workshop I was conducting. A mom said to me, "I can't help my child with his homework anymore."

Her child was only in third grade, and I could see years of parent support disappearing if she gave up now. "Why don't you think you can help?" I asked.

"I can't do algebra," said the mom. "He's doing algebra already and I don't know how."

"If I show you a way to do algebra, do you think that might help?" I asked.

She nodded, but I could tell she was sure I couldn't get her to understand algebra. I asked if her son was doing multiplication in third grade. When she said yes, I asked her to give me the answer to "two times three equals blank." Without hesitating, she answered correctly. Then I asked what went in the blank for "two times blank equals six." She gave the correct answer again. Next I asked her to solve for "a" in the equation "two times 'a' equals six."

She looked startled then started to smile, a real smile of understanding. "It's three. I get it. I can do algebra!"

Many parents don't know they can help. They lack the confidence or the knowledge that they have the necessary skills. As you get to know the parents, you will be able to point out their strengths and show them how to use them to teach their children. Their confidence will increase as they see their children progressing. Soon they will be comfortable asking you for new ways to help their children. That's a big step and it's about that trust we mentioned earlier, the trust you've been developing for awhile now.

You're Not Through Yet

You might think, *Whew, parents are coming into school and they're getting the idea they can help at home. Great. I'm done here; it's time to go back to dealing with budgets and test scores.*

I'm here to tell you your role isn't finished. In fact it's just starting. You'll need a process to identify areas where parent capacity is already strong as well as those areas in need. The discussions, meetings, and visits with your parents will help determine the areas of greatest strength and those of greatest need. As you get to know parents, survey them for their perceived strengths and needs. Below are a couple of examples and a format for deciding where to start.

In one school community, parents may have indicated these needs and strengths:

Needs	*Strengths*
Poor Reading Skills	Most have gardens
Not many books at home	Families like to cook
Don't read to children	Women sew/do needlework
Fear of being embarrassed about reading	Men fish
Not all are fluent in English	Know history of families
Want children to read	Tell stories

Summarize your findings in a few words, as shown in the previous list. Then indicate on a scale of zero to ten where you believe the strengths and needs are for the families in your area. Ten being a highest strength, zero being a highest need, and DK for don't know. When you have a DK, it's time to have more conversations. You'll need to know about all the areas as you plan your strategies. Next, using a chart such as the one shown on the next page, write the strengths and needs into a grid that matches your curriculum areas.

This is your estimation and, although accurate for you, it may or may not be accurate from the view of other school staff and parents. You may not actually show parents your chart, but ask or observe to see if your perception is accurate. If reading is a ten, ask parents with whom you have a good relationship about building reading capacity. Would they like to be able to read stories to their children? What stories would they like to read? Ask the teachers who work with the children and who are talking with the parents. Ask the parents who are coming to your coffees and tours. Observe their reading skills when you ask them to read an agenda or a story to a child in a classroom. Check to see if your observations are accurate. Assure each group that, as you recognize areas of need, together you will be designing ways to help build those skills.

If you have a very skilled group of parents in the area of reading, ask other questions. How do they support their children's reading? Would they like to share their favorite books or stories with a class? Are they interested in helping in the library or with a Reader's Theater? Recognize and build on the strengths in the community.

Reading	Math	Science	Social Studies	Arts and Leisure
Mentioned as concern/fear	Not mentioned	Gardens	Recognize history	Sewing
Don't have skills or materials	Need more information	Cooking	Know own background	Needlework
Hard Don't do it		Fishing		
1	DK	7	3	7

In another community, you might find a chart like this:

Reading	Math	Science	Social Studies	Arts and Leisure
Avid readers	Number of professional people	Parks nearby	Live away from where grew up	Little time
Go to library regularly	Many CEOs, accountants	Very busy, go occasionally	Too busy to spend time with older family members	Both of us work Don't have time for hobbies
Highly skilled		Don't think about it much		
10	9	4	2	1

Once you have a clearer picture of your community's areas of need, you may notice those needs correspond to your test scores. It's time to take some action. Research is clear that one of the best ways to build skills is to train for the skills you want. Joyce Epstein (2005) reports, "…the differences in whether parents believe they should help or can help are shaped by what the school and the teachers do. For example, if teachers want parents to think they should help, teachers must demonstrate this with an active program of parent involvement in learning activities at home. If teachers want parents to feel confident they can help, teachers and administrators must organize and conduct workshops for parents on how to help."

Demonstrate, demonstrate, demonstrate, (and did I mention demonstrate?) the skills you want parents to use. When you take on a new job, it's normal to expect someone to show you how to do the work. You want to know how to mop the floors, how to file the papers, or what color the house and trim are supposed to be. The same applies to what you'd like parents to do with learning. Handing them a packet of papers with the expectation they will do it the way you want is like handing someone a paintbrush and telling them to paint your house. You might end up with an unfinished candy-striped house in purple and magenta. They painter could be quite disappointed and surprised when you rant, rave, and refuse to pay. You might realize, when you finally draw a breath, you never gave any direction about what you wanted. Don't expect the parents in your school to provide reading support just because you hand them a book.

Your best trainers, or direction-providers, are the teachers at your school. Teachers are the obvious ones to carry out a program for helping children learn. Teachers are also the ones to benefit from the results. Of course, the children benefit from parents who are reading to them, teaching them how to count beans for soup, or creating science experiments with them. And the parents get the benefit of refreshing old skills or learning new ones as well as the benefit of spending time with their children. Teachers can directly see the benefits in their classroom as children come to school with more skills, enthusiasm, and interest. When parents are engaged with the learning at home, it shows.

Dr. Joni says...

√   Provide opportunities for learning.

√   Focus on the strengths, not on deficits.

√   Build confidence and relationships to build capacity.

Chapter V

C — Collaborate for Success

Collaborating on a project allows people to get to know each other, develop trust, and gain appreciation for one another. The collaborative group should identify a need, develop a plan to address the need, and execute the plan.

Many parents don't come to school to help because of their own experiences when they were children. Perhaps they didn't do well, got in trouble, or failed a class. They may still feel inadequate in a school setting. Or, like Elio, maybe they never went to school. Parents need to know school is a safe place where they will not be hurt or rejected, and where they are valued. Collaborative efforts allow parents and school staff to develop trust as they work on simple projects like fixing a leaky water fountain or sprucing up the front entrance to the school.

Sounds easy, but why do it? You could hire someone to do either one of those activities or assign them to the janitor. You could. But the purpose of the collaborative is for everyone to be involved and valued in the process. The project planning and design requires listening, talking, cooperating, and being surprised at the skills others have. And that's where attitudes begin to shift.

"Wow, I thought those parents couldn't do anything, but you should have seen Jack and Carlos fix that water fountain. They knew what they were doing."

And the other side of that coin, "Wow, the teachers liked what we did with the water fountain. They were so grateful. I wonder if there's something else we could do?"

As the level of trust, respect, and confidence increases between teachers and parents, collaboration begins in earnest. Make decisions and develop plans for meeting physical needs around the school, and for meeting the educational needs of the children.

No Buy-in, No Collaboration

Suppose a developer decides to build a project in the middle of a pasture because there's plenty of space and he thinks this would be a great place to put up a building. The building may sit empty because no one else saw a need for a building there.

Now, if the citizens of a town decide they need and want a place to meet, they will know what they need, how many rooms it should have, and what functions they will hold in it. They will go to planning meetings to make sure the future building meets their needs, and they will find the funds to finance construction.

Only then will they hire a developer to build the structure they want in the location they've chosen.

Schools can be like the building in the middle of the pasture or the centrally located town hall. When the citizens collaborated on the town hall, they felt an ownership because they had a part in planning a facility that would meet their needs.

Schools have often worked as isolated silos in the pastures, teaching alone and apart from other sections of the community. Parents often don't have a clue how their children go off to first grade in September knowing a few letters of their names, and come home at the end of the year reading sentences from books. Or, how third graders start the year with only a mastery of addition and subtraction, but can multiply and divide by the spring. Parents watch their sophomores sign up for driver's education classes and wonder how it happened that the family car is no longer in the driveway. It's a mystery.

Parents leave teachers in the silos to do their work, accepting the separation as the status quo. They stay out of the way. Oh, they come in for periodic updates, like a yearly physical, but for the most part, they don't participate.

A school that uses P-TAG Step A (Attitude) and Step B (Building Capacity) to engage parents chips away the silo-thinking and moves parents closer to feeling ownership with the daily process of education.

Step C, the "Collaborate for Success" stage, requires an open, accepting attitude where everyone is valued and heard. A collaborative effort will continue building the capacity you started developing in Step B. You're not finished with Steps A and B. They are ongoing throughout the P-TAG process. Step C continues to build relationships. You began those relationships by getting to know the parents in the community. You extended your relationships by providing engagement activities. Parents are coming to your school, having coffee, helping with projects, and are willing to be there.

Now you're ready to engage a number of parents and teachers into a collaborative group to focus on a specific outcome. During this step, you build another level of trust, confidence, and capacity for parents, teachers, support staff, and administrators.

You will ask staff and parents to work together on a project. It doesn't have to be a huge project. A first project might be something simple like renovating the front pick-up and drop-off area, re-organizing the lunch program supervision, or providing a movie night once a month. Choose a project of high interest. Choose a finite project. Choose a project where all participants can be valued for their involvement.

It is best to choose a first project that requires little budget support and for which you or the district leadership have little or no required or preconceived outcomes. Yes, you want to fix a real problem, but more importantly for this step, you want to build parent engagement, trust, and confidence. The first adventure into collaboration needs to be successful.

Start with teachers and parents who wish to be involved. Describe the project, indicate any timelines, let people know how long you think it might take to meet and make some decisions. Then, set up a first meeting at a convenient time for parents and teachers. You may need to provide childcare or translators. Parent participation can count toward volunteer hours. Teacher participation can be part of their school day or take the place of a mandatory staff meeting. You'll want people to be involved and interested, not distracted with where else they need to be.

Murphy School's Collaborative Project

The Murphy School District in inner city Phoenix, Arizona, was ready for one of those larger projects. Murphy staff spent several years building a welcoming, engaging environment for parents. Each of their schools had a resource center where parents could meet, enjoy coffee, and get to know each other as they prepared items for an upcoming carnival or took classes to improve their English.

Parents in the Head Start program at Murphy had a long history of being involved in decision making through the parent policy council and through participation in the preschool classroom. However, collaboration between the Head Start preschool program and the kindergarten, the first grade, and the second grade programs was almost non-existent, even though the Head Start classrooms and the K-2 building were on the same school site. The two were operated by different entities, controlled by different funding sources and mandates, and the teachers didn't know each other. Parents coming from Head Start stated they didn't get the same reception or opportunities for engagement in grade K-2 that they received in Head Start. The district leadership decided to change the whole dynamic.

They invited three district level administrators, two principals, two teachers, two Head Start staff members, two Family Resource employees, and two parents to design a vision, mission statement, and goals for a preschool to K-2 collaboration. They received a grant for funds, but the focus was not on the grant as much as it was on the process of collaboration to make learning more cohesive, a system that all participants could share in and understand.

Administrators were committed to the project because they had applied for and accepted the grant funds; but the superintendent, as well as those on the committee, wanted the parents to be involved in the project. Principals volunteered and teachers were given release days with substitutes. Head Start staff members also committed because of the grant. Family Resource Center staff was there to represent the parent perspective as well as support the parents in the group.

Getting Started on Your Project

Once you've chosen a project and have a group commitment, it's time for your first meeting. Pick a date and time convenient for those attending. Don't forget the childcare or translators. Reduce as many barriers as possible so all who are attending can participate easily. Translation is often a large barrier. This includes translation into the parents' native languages as well as keeping *educationese* out of the discussion as much as possible.

Color Coded Personalities

There will be various personalities at the meeting. You'll have the ones I call the reds — "let's get the job done, I've got lots to do and we have a task that needs to be accomplished so let's get on with it." Administrators are often the reds, but other group members may be also.

You'll have the blue personalities — "I want this to feel good and right, I need lots of time to talk about it, touch it, and taste it before I'm ready to move on." These folks drive the reds crazy. Reassuring the reds that the job will be done, and supporting the blue's need-to-process is a delicate balancing act.

You'll have the grays – they like to blend into the background. You may never hear their opinion, and they may leave the room without saying anything. These are often the first ones to have things to say back at their school or in the community. Bring them out by encouraging them to share throughout the process.

You'll have the oranges – they like to throw out their opinion because they have one and will then sit back and watch others react. Let them be heard, but make sure they can also hear others who agree and/or disagree without malice. They'll need to see some of their opinions adopted while others disappear.

Value each opinion without judgment and engage each as often as possible. The art and act of connecting with those in the group allows the development of trust, support, and teamwork. Remember, collaboration is your first priority.

Collaboration IS in the Details

Explain the project to the group. Describe what the task is and if there are any restrictions. Your comments may go something like this:

"Most of our drinking fountains are cracked or broken. We've repaired them until they can't be repaired anymore. We have two hundred dollars in the budget allocated for fixing them. We want kids, especially at recess, to have water to drink. We need to figure out what to do."

For educators this may sound like a Problem Based Learning (PBL) strategy. If you're not familiar with PBL, Barbara Duch (University of Delaware Website) describes it as "an instructional method that challenges students to 'learn to learn,' working cooperatively in groups to seek solutions to real world problems." In our case, your "students" are parents and teachers learning to learn.

Your collaborative process is very similar, and like students using PBL, you'll want folks to work through possible answers, come up with the most feasible ones, and find something that works. You may need to provide those in your collaborative with team-building or shared-decision making strategies. While new skills are important, your major focus for this first project is for the group to become comfortable sharing their ideas and getting to know one another. Often group members will find themselves using talents they didn't recognize they had to solve problems.

Encourage the group to discuss the problem. Talk about why the fountains are broken, how they got that way, and how long they've been broken. This is the "what is" stage — the reality of the way it is right now. Some in the group will need time to process the situation. Some may want to stay at this stage, complaining about how it got that way or whose fault it might be. It's part of their processing. Those folks may also wish to stay in the "what is" stage because they don't have answers to fix the problem and would rather not move on. That's allowed for a bit, but don't stay stuck there.

Collaboration Requires a Common Vision

Go to stage two, the "what we want it to be" stage. This is a critical piece where a common vision is developed. This is not the solution stage. Solutions come later. This is where each member helps develop a picture of what the group wants.

Give your water fountain collaborative group time to create a picture of children at recess running, playing, getting thirsty, and wanting a drink of water. Allow group members to envision children happily quenching their thirst after their play. What does this scene look like? What are the children doing? How do they get the water they need? What pictures come to mind? Write down the descriptors the members provide. Use their descriptions of what they envision to create a composite picture of an ideal situation.

Murphy School District Collaborative wanted to create vision and mission statements. The vision statement was their collaborative's concept of what they wanted for the preschool to grade three children in the district. Administrators had several ideas — high test scores, meeting proficiencies, students entering higher grades capable of succeeding and graduating. Head Start Administrators wanted preschoolers to feel confident, capable, and sure of themselves so they could tackle any new subject or situation. Teachers wanted children to learn and enjoy what they taught in class. Family Resource Specialists wanted parents to participate and feel a part of the decision-making process for their children. Parents wanted to know their children were cared for and helped to learn and be successful. Each had a slightly different picture of a vision for their preschool to third grade children. Each brought different values, thoughts, and ideas.

The Murphy collaborative spent time talking about what they wanted for their children. They developed a vision board with each member cutting pictures from magazines that looked like what they wanted. Their vision board came alive as they placed their pictures on it. Together they created a common picture. Only then did they choose words and phrases for their vision statement.

It takes time to allow all ideas to emerge. The Murphy collaborative actions included their vision board process and their discussions about values, personal issues, and concerns. Sometimes those issues had nothing to do with the project at hand. Those off-task discussions were noted, valued, and accepted. As people recognized and understood that this was not the avenue for all issues, they could return to the project at hand.

Their final vision statement not only addressed the desires of the group, but also literally brought a picture to mind! The vision board moved participants' ideas into a concrete representation each member could easily describe. Their final vision statement was *Hand in Hand Together for More.*

Back to Your Project

Your water fountain collaborative will need a common picture in order to come up with solutions that work. Often we go from a problem directly to any solution that looks like it will fix the immediate issue. The administrator hires a plumber, but with only two hundred dollars in the budget, the work is shoddy and the leaks are back in a few weeks. Teachers tell the students to bring water bottles because the fountains don't work, but some students forget, others can't afford them, and some water bottles are lost or children fight over which one belongs to them. Settling water bottle disputes takes more time than teaching math.

Both are good solutions and quick to fix a problem, but the result may cause more problems. Starting with a picture of the result you want, the vision of the outcome, leads to better solutions.

Imagine children coming back to class after recess, refreshed, and ready to learn. That picture makes finding a solution easier for your group. With a common picture in your mind, your group can talk about solutions.

Generate a number of possibilities. Write them down. Value each. Discuss each. Discuss the pros and cons of each until you can agree on the best plan of action for your situation. You have reached the "what we're going to do about reaching our vision" stage.

Murphy's Next Steps

Murphy's collaborative took the time and did the work. They created their vision board and vision statement and continued their discussions to develop a mission statement before they went to goals.

Murphy's mission statement read, "The Murphy School District Community will develop and support a welcoming environment where communication and relationships foster language and literacy to promote high levels of success for the early childhood experience and beyond."

Their group formed a strong bond at all levels. Their statement created another word picture that let everyone know what they wanted to do. Only then did they move to solutions/goals describing how they were going to accomplish their vision. You'll see how to develop a plan of action that works in the next chapter, but in this stage, we are building the collaboration skills necessary to work together toward a common goal.

Collaboration Requires Patience

Yes, the process takes more time. It certainly would be easier and quicker to patch together the drinking fountains you have or hire the plumber. But the purpose of this project is not only to get the drinking fountains fixed, but also to include parents and teachers in a collaborative effort to solve a problem. Remember, you wanted to see how engagement works and to connect parents and teachers at a different level.

The goal of Step C, collaboration, is to develop relationships and a level of trust that will allow you to take on more and more complex issues. Asking parents to rewrite policy or tackle the bus schedule is often beyond what anyone is interested in or capable of doing without a good deal of prior knowledge. Without the skills to do the job, the task becomes frustrating and folks don't show up; or worse, due to their frustration, they lose confidence in themselves and in you. They take it out by talking to everyone they know about how poorly things are run in THAT school.

When the collaborative project is accomplished, the group members feel like they contributed to the school. Trust and relationships are strengthened, and become the springboard to academic activities.

The ultimate goal for future collaboration is to engage parents in their children's learning both at school and at home. They will be able to do take-home learning activities when they feel comfortable, valued, capable, and part of the learning team. If they can see the value in fixing the drinking fountain, they've participated in the solution to a school issue. They see the results. Your job will be easier when you ask them not only to recommend ways to fix the fountain but also to participate in the classroom or read with their child at home. They see the results when they fix the fountain. Then they see the results when they participate in helping their child learn the alphabet or the multiplication tables. This is the "what can be" vision that progresses through determining your goals and moving toward them.

Murphy's Goals

The Murphy District Collaborative finished their vision and mission statements, created a number of goals, and developed activities and timelines to accomplish their plans. Members of the collaborative went to other schools in the district and shared the program they developed. Armed with the vision board, popcorn, and a video of their collaborative effort, they held joint staff meetings between Head Start and K-8 staff across the district. This was the first time some of the staff had ever met each other. The collaborative members, including parents, explained their goals and their progress so far. After their success at staff meetings, members of the collaborative formed a subcommittee to monitor the progress.

This adventure proved so successful for Murphy that they took the next step. When it was time to revise their district's mission and vision statements, they again invited parents, teachers, and administrators to participate. They moved from a focused, finite, successful project to a district-wide plan. This time the vision was even more successful. Five parents served on the team. Three were non-English speakers. The result was a vision statement the whole district could be proud of: *Educational Success Today to Achieve Tomorrow's Future.*

Collaboration Brings About New Experiences

These are new experiences for members of any school collaborative. It's new for administrators to invest the time in parents. It's new for teachers to work jointly with administrators and parents, make district-wide decisions, and then take responsibility for implementation and success. It's new for parents to feel their voices are heard and their ideas implemented.

Collaboration is a People Process

In Step C, you built collaborative relationships. You started those relationships as you assessed attitudes and engaged with parents over coffee. You listened to parents' histories, interests, and dreams. And, you discovered their talents and skills, and how they think and process information.

If you've picked a project that is open to creative answers, you'll get much more from the process of discovering how others think and act than you will from solving the problem. The custodian can always fix the water fountains again, but when you come to know how people process and create, you'll know more about how your community works and thinks. Your future projects will be easier and even more successful.

Dr. Joni says...

- √ Start with a vision!
- √ Anticipate the need for patience and acceptance.
- √ Get out of the silo and into the town square.

CHAPTER VI

D — DEVELOP A PLAN

Every novel has a plot and characters to carry it out. Every movie has a story line with main and supporting actors. Every TV episode has a script to give the cast direction. An hour of *Law and Order* goes from a crime to an arrest to a trial to a verdict. Jack McCoy doesn't leave the courtroom without the wrap-up to a case. In all those shows, nothing happens without a script and a cast. Each cast member contributes to the successes of the show. Some parts are bigger than others are, but none is insignificant.

Developing and implementing a plan for your school is a lot like getting each skilled person following a well-designed script for the success of the show.

Your first reaction may be, "Wait, I'm not a screenwriter or director, and the tasks are huge. I can't create a show, especially one that includes characters — parents — who are extras to the school scene."

Let me assure you that you can create such a show, and those extras will make or break your whole play. You orchestrate the script for the students in your school every day. You decide what goes on in the classroom. You write the plan. You know the short and long-term objectives you want. You make it happen — directing and acting both. Think about it. You are good at it. But, you haven't looked at it in that light before.

So, if you can do it for students, you can do it with the parents too, and you can do it with outstanding results. Now, let's talk about how.

Review Your Project Success

In the last chapter, you considered an area of need, and then you formed a collaborative to create and carry out a project to meet that need. It could have been the drinking fountains or establishing a vision statement. Although the project results were important, they were not the ultimate goal. The goal was to develop relationships between teachers and parents. You were developing levels of mutual trust, but project completion was the visible outcome.

You accomplished your objective. Both the people involved and the community were able to see the results of your efforts. Participants in the collaborative learned they were valuable cast members, and their success has other parents considering a part in the next projects. Your work is beginning to grow. Growth is part of the result of building your collaborative.

Next Project: A Learning Activity

The verb form of school is "to train or educate." The noun form is "an institution for teaching children." Often our initial projects take the form of fixing the noun form. We fix the faucets. We fix a lifeless wall by painting a mural on it. We fix a parking problem in the bus lot. Somehow, it's easier to *fix the institution* than it is to take on the verb form, training or educating. My own guess for why it's easier to work with teachers and parents on the institution than on education, is that most of us educators spent a great deal of time in classes learning how to teach. It's a little hard on our egos to think someone else might be capable of doing what we worked so hard to learn. If we share or give away what we have, then we don't hold the key anymore. We would no longer be the keeper of the knowledge or the guru of guidance. It's a hard thing to give up control, but that is what we need to do. To encourage a knowledgeable community of parents, we need to include others in the processes of learning, teaching, and educating.

Let's look at a basic skill area and see how we can get parents on board as supporting cast members. Our plot for this episode might include parents and educators working together to design a plan for increasing the reading skills of kindergarten through second grade readers. Wow, what would that do to your test scores? Imagine the confidence children would have when they begin third grade fully capable of handling any reading activity for the year. Imagine those same children in sixth grade or eleventh grade still being able to read at their grade level. Now that's a successful vision!

Generate the Excitement

Bring together an early elementary collaborative of administrators, teachers, and parents, and give them the desired outcome of the new project: to have all children leave second grade reading with a high degree of confidence, skill, understanding, and fluency. This is like a Problem-Based Learning (PBL) project you might give to seventh graders studying Medieval History. They are to trace their ancestors back and develop a coat of arms depicting those areas they found in their families' backgrounds. The seventh graders become excited about what they find as they explore their backgrounds — robbers, barons, and robber barons show up and the coat of arms begins to emerge.

Your collaborative members will be equally excited when they understand how students learn to read, what teaching strategies will help improve reading, and how their assistance will influence the learning of not only their own children, but also all children in their school.

Start with the excitement. In your script for the seventh graders Medieval projects, you might have created the vision for the end project by giving examples of what others have done or showing Internet pictures of coats of arms from famous families. Build the excitement of your reading collaborative by sharing stories from children who have become avid readers and their delight in what they read. Have a third grade child, who is a fluent reader, read a story to the group. Give them a tangible target — a vision. Create a picture for them to work toward.

Personal Stakes

The triad membership of parents, teachers, and administrators has a purpose. Administrators will bring their desire for children to be proficient to the table, but will also help identify legal issues and monetary support for collaborative plans. Teachers will share best practices to teach reading, as well as their desire for this project to succeed since it supports classroom curriculum. Parents have skills, energy, and daily access to their children as well as their desire to see their children reading anything from recipes to directions for setting up the DVD. You now have the people and their desire to help. Desires will drive and sustain motivation when things bog down.

Administrators, teachers, and parents all have stakes in any plan or project they are involved with. These interests may sustain folks until the project is complete, but if some children don't respond to the plan, a teacher isn't supportive, or a parent doesn't find time to help, a deeper motivation is called for. The beginning of a project is the time to discover and share the personal reasons why the project is important to your collaborative members.

Once the group gets to know each other and decides on their project, set aside one session to talk about why this project is important to each member. A mom's desire for her son to read may not only come from wanting him to graduate and go to college. It may be because mom is dyslexic or never got past the third grade in school. She sees how difficult life is because she can't read. A teacher may teach reading because she was an only child whose parents both worked and her best and only friends were the storybook characters she knew.

Motivators like these will keep people collaborating toward their goals when they've had a long day and don't want to go to a meeting or they don't like the materials the state has given them to teach reading this year, or whatever else might intervene in their progress. These intrinsic motivators are the reasons why each person is in the collaborative working toward a goal of K-2 reading success. Encourage members to acknowledge their own motivators as well as those of others.

Vision Board and Statement

Now, as with your collaborative institution projects, develop a common vision for your learning project. Create a vision board on tag board or on a bulletin board using pictures cut from a magazine; or have an artistic member of your collaborative draw a composite picture of what the group envisions as the product. Perhaps you'll have pictures of children checking books out of the library, children reading to their preschool siblings, or children completing a reading incentive program and holding their certificates. The collaborative's vision sets the possibilities and there are no limits. This vision board becomes the visual reminder of what you want your children to achieve by the end of this process. Place the vision board in a prominent place in your school so not only the collaborative, but also others in the community can see what you're doing.

Next, work on a vision statement based on your vision board. Make the statement short, easy to remember, and meaningful. For this learning project, it might be *Roaring Readers K-2.*

Your Mission

Determining your mission is the next order of business. What does the collaborative want to accomplish? Why do they want to accomplish that? For your institutional projects, the collaborative takes on things like drinking fountains. The mission is to fix all the drinking fountains in the school, so the children are refreshed and ready to learn.

For your learning project, the collaborative asks the same questions. For example, a school might support the reading process for kindergarteners through second graders, so all of those students in the regular education program will read at or above grade level by the end of second grade.

Let's Get More Specific

Your vision and mission lead you to goals and specific objectives. Goals are usually broad, while objectives are much more specific. For example, the overall goal may be as simple as all children will read at their grade level. Objectives are more specific, measurable steps that lead up to the goal, and are often sequential in nature.

Let's create a hypothetical school — we'll call it Lincoln School — and look at objectives that their collaborative might create to meet the reading goal:

Goal: All children will read at grade level.

Objectives:

Kindergarten - All Kindergarten children will:

√ Name all the letters of the alphabet and sounds of the

alphabet
- √ Read one hundred words by sight
- √ Listen to fifty books by the end of the school year

First grade - All first grade children will:
- √ Know all vowels and blends
- √ Sound out simple words
- √ Read one thousand words by sight
- √ Read fifty books aloud by the end of the year

Second grade - All second grade children will:
- √ Decode new words, including nonsense words, with sounds they know
- √ Read fifty grade-level books either aloud or silently
- √ Demonstrate comprehension by discussing the books read

Support

These are skills directly related to the standards taught at each grade level. Teachers will support these objectives with instruction, and will measure progress through classroom and annual standardized evaluations. Administrators will support these objectives since reading is one of the highest academic directives of an elementary school.

Will parents support this goal and these objectives? They will if they helped to create them. They will if the school acknowledges their support as a valuable contribution to the education of their children. Student goals become important to parents when they have participated in the decision-making and delivery of services.

For some members of the collaborative, the vision-mission-goals-objectives development is enough to spur them into action. Teachers in the collaborative change their lessons plans and add an extra half hour to the reading schedule. Parents head to the library with their book lists in hand. Although their activities may be beneficial for the children they touch, the collaborative mission says all children will be reading at grade level — not only the ones whose parents are part of the collaborative. The need is for all K-2 to be engaged — administrators, teachers, support staff, parents, and children. To reach all of them, specific activities must be set up so all parents and staff members can participate in the reading success.

Implementation

One activity might be a daily twenty-minute sustained reading time. In kindergarten and first grade, the teachers read a story aloud during that time. Elsewhere, administrators, teachers, aides, and students, are reading silently. The activity is a twenty-minute-a-day reading session. Timelines indicate when this activity is going to happen and for how long. Daily reading from 11:30 to 11:50 AM will begin the first day of September and continue until May 30.

Now we need a home activity. At my house, we read by pages. I had four children at different reading levels. Beginning in third grade, each child read at least one hundred pages of something he or she was interested in per week. We set aside time to read to or with our children after dinner and before bedtime.

Perhaps your collaborative will suggest a family reading activity of fifty pages a week for each early elementary child. Early elementary books are very short, contain few words, have many pictures, and allow success for limited readers, whether children or parents. For parents who haven't read with their children before, you may schedule a session with a librarian or a teacher who can build capacity by demonstrating techniques like being animated and excited about the story, telling stories about the pictures in a book, or asking good questions about a favorite story.

Extrinsic Motivation

For motivation, your collaborative might want to put a sign up for the number of books each classroom has read or give prizes for those who read fifty pages a week for a month. Your group can decide what will work best in your school. Be specific. Demonstrate what you want, build-in excitement, and value the results.

You'll notice in each of these examples there's a measurable objective: to read a certain amount of time or pages at home; an activity (reading alone or with an adult in the home), and, a timeline for when it will occur (daily or weekly). The objectives, activities to support the objectives, and timelines help you document what the collaborative wishes to accomplish, and provide the data to measure progress toward their goal. Teacher checklists and home reading logs are two tools that can track family reading time. Also, an accomplishment brag-board is a strong motivator for students and parents to follow through at home.

Key Players

Your group needs key players on the stage. There are those who coordinate, those who motivate and energize, those who sell or carry your message, and those who do the quiet behind-the-scenes work of making sure you meet the objectives. You need all of these players. And you'll need to monitor who's doing what. It's easy to develop a plan only to find no one is actually carrying it out. It's important to designate a coordinator to oversee progress and provide help when needed. An administrator or designated parent liaison makes a good coordinator, but anyone in your group may take on the role. At collaborative meetings, the coordinator may ask the members to report on the actions they have taken since the last meeting, share any problems they've encountered, and tell what they are planning next.

When the collaborative members meet, they'll want to know if they are on target with their goals. St. Hope Elementary's parent involvement hours are a good example for creating an objective, an action, a timeline, and an evaluation. Their goal was to include parents in school activities. They created an objective to have each parent in the school volunteer at least forty hours during the school year. Their parent coordinator was responsible for providing activities the parents could do as well as to track the hours.

In 2003-04, 70 percent of the St. Hope parents provided forty hours. It took time for the culture and the value of their involvement to take hold, but by 2007-08, 98 percent of the parents were participating and many were doing more than forty hours of volunteer time per year. In addition, over the five years, their state test scores increased from 638 to 802, an amazing jump for an inner city low-income school. Actions were tracked, valued, evaluated, and shared. So were the results.

Money, Money, Money

Developing a plan requires reviewing which items have a price tag and which ones won't require a budgetary expenditure. Your plan needs to identify what costs are involved and how to meet those costs.

Let's say your plan to read to children is set and the collaborative is ready to move on it, but the classrooms don't have books to lend. They only have the state curriculum materials. The library at the school can help, but it's small and only allows children to check out one book a week. Some families have books at home, others don't. Families may have books but not at a beginning reader's ability level. Your collaborative wants books.

Budget concerns are one reason to have an administrator on the collaborative. He or she can quickly let you know if there is money budgeted for your particular needs. Lack of funding is not a reason to stop your plan, however. The collaborative will need to be as creative in meeting budgetary needs as developing their plan. A thirty thousand dollar request for books probably won't happen, but a three thousand dollar grant may be available through district funds. Three thousand dollars could go a long way toward finding books at garage sales or for printing non-copyrighted beginning level reading materials. Requesting donations or having fundraisers can be part of the collaborative's action plan if they know funding will be an issue. It's all part of developing a plan and implementing it. Being realistic and still asking for the best possible outcome are not mutually exclusive activities.

Engaging Parents

Your collaborative has created a great plan. You identified your vision, mission, goals, and objectives. You developed the action steps and timelines and included an evaluation component. Are you feeling tired? Let's bring in some reinforcements.

The actors and the extras have been waiting for the script to be complete. It's time to include others in your show. Identify who else can help you complete your plan. In the plan to make *Roaring Readers* K-2, all the K-2 teachers are potential partners. Not all may be on the collaborative, but all will greatly benefit from the results of this plan. The parents of the children in K-2 are also partners and you want them to be reading at home as well. Your collaborative's task now is to engage more cooperation.

Analyze ways to increase participation. It may be through your teachers' communication with parents, the school newsletter, a workshop, or potluck at school where you share the plan. A parent back-to-school night or parent conferences are great places to make sure teachers and parents share information, provide reading activities, or demonstrate how to read a book. Your collaborative can select the best vehicles for your sharing.

If you are your collaborative's coordinator, be prepared for the on-going communication and support the collaborative will need to continue its work. Members need to know what the community is doing to support their efforts. They'll want to know what the teachers say about the reading progress in the staff meetings. They'll want to see the results in the school newsletter and have it reported at a board meeting. Their results are personal. They've put time and effort into this and they want to know what's happening. Let's show them…

Dr. Joni says…

√   Identify key players and identify your mission.
√   Set your goals and determine your plan of action.
√   Generate excitement!

CHAPTER VII

E — EVALUATE PROGRESS

Every plan needs a check-up. If weight loss is a goal, then the scale is the tool to evaluate the progress. You have a vision for what you will look like when you lose weight. You have an eating and exercise plan. You're following your plan closely. The scale shows slow but steady progress toward your new weight.

Similar occurrences will happen with the collaborative learning plan. When you've jointly agreed on an action and you've diligently carried it out, you will see positive results. Test scores will increase. Attendance will increase. Behavioral referrals will go down and support from families will rise. Yes, that's what you wanted and it feels good.

Sometimes, however, you'll reach a plateau or an especially stubborn stage where nothing seems to happen. Your collaborative has tapped into one of those festering sores and the plan becomes bogged down. Sometimes you will need to revise your plan, go back to your planning team, or talk about what is working and what isn't.

During these plateaus in progress, it is important to strengthen the trust you have established. It is not the time to blame anyone for not making planned progress. If there are areas of difficulty, explore what will help them get back on track. You may need an outside source to review data and progress, and to kick-start your collaborative back into its positive mode. Again, avoid blame. That will only defeat what you are trying to create.

We evaluate situations and make decisions based on those evaluations everyday. Walk into an ice-cream shop and vanilla, chocolate, and strawberry call for a decision. Maybe it's a vanilla day for you. And, for me? I'll take straw…, no, I'll have chocolate. We decide between the freeway and the scenic route. We choose to walk to work or drive the car. We are constantly evaluating actions and making decisions based on our evaluation.

Our knowledge, or the data we have about a situation, influences our evaluation, but that is only part of the process. The other part is emotion. Data tells me I get headaches from chocolate, but I love the taste. I want it so I'll take my chances. My GPS tells me the freeway is shorter, but I like the trees along the back road. My scale says I could use the walk, but I'm afraid I'll be late. Data and emotions sway my decisions. Sometimes data wins out, but often the emotions will overrule logic. I enjoy my drive down the back road with a chocolate ice cream cone.

Evaluation is part of any program in our schools. We're educated folks, taught with scientific methodology in our coursework, and filled with the admonitions reminding us to rely on the current research.

We receive and collect data in our schools to make research-based decisions. We have quizzes, chapter tests, written work, report cards, and state yearly assessments. We have attendance sheets, referral forms, and numbers of retainees and graduates. We have budgets, quarterly reports, and annual monitoring of programs. We have tons of data to help evaluate what we're doing. The data shows us what we're doing, but it doesn't show us how we're feeling about the situation or project.

Parents Know How School Feels

Parents don't always come with scientific or research backgrounds, but they know how school feels. It feels good when they walk into the office and the secretary greets them. It feels good when they visit the first grade classroom and Mrs. Jones is teaching reading. It feels bad in the cafeteria when the students bolt their food down to have more time for recess before the next period.

The parents may not react to the data about how many hours of training the secretary had to learn front desk procedures. Nor do they care that Mrs. Jones is a highly qualified teacher with thirty-four graduate level units. Nor do they realize that to comply with the number of minutes required in a school day, including play times, there's little choice but to rush the kids through lunch. What matters to the parents is whether school feels good or bad, comfortable or not, easy or hard. And, if we are truthful, how we feel about our jobs and the progress our students are making is probably more important to us than the data is!

Our evaluation tools must take into account both how we're doing and how we're feeling — head and heart. So with that in mind let's see what we need to evaluate our P-TAG learning collaborative.

Make Results Visual

The goal for the collaborative at Lincoln School was to promote reading at grade level by third grade for all children. Activities included a daily reading time in school and parents reading with their children at home. Throughout the project, the team will collect data. They may include the data in the newsletter so all the parents and staff are aware of progress.

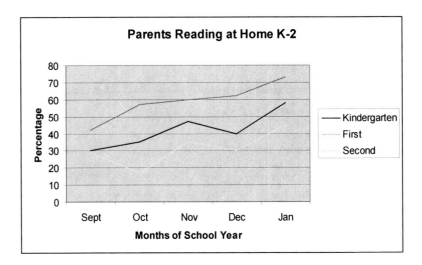

They may use a simple chart, like the one above, to show how many parents are reading to their children at home from each of the grades. Using the data in a visual way helps everyone see what's going on and it feels like everything is on track to bring about the success intended.

Perhaps your collaborative hasn't kept data. Perhaps you haven't even thought about keeping it. Look around. You have data now that helps support progress toward your activities. You planned to buy books so parents could read at home. How many have you bought? How many go out weekly? You have data. You'll need to bring it together to show what you're doing. If it isn't as thorough as you'd like, develop a system of collecting information that will give you a clearer picture. You can track numbers of books, time spent in reading at school, pages of books read at home.

Your collaborative members, as well as your community, need to see those kinds of results. It's like the Jerry Lewis telethons for Muscular Dystrophy. You can see the numbers go up. People get involved and excited because the telethon results are visible, but the real goal is to cure the problem.

The collaborative, teachers, and parents want to see the charts and track the data because it's fun and exciting to watch the numbers climb, but the ultimate goal is to have all children reading at grade level. To do that you'll need to look farther. Your collaborative will need to look at additional data and analyze who needs more specific treatment and support in order to meet your real goal for ALL students.

But Wait There's More

Deeper areas to assess include attendance, behavior, grades, and test results.

Children attend school for many reasons — parents make them go, it's where their friends are, everyone goes to school, it's warm and there's food, and it's fun. There may be many reasons not to show-up — it's hard, there's no way to succeed, there are no friends, it's dangerous, and it produces failure. Attitude is everything and the welcoming environment from Step A in our process comes through as loudly for students as it does for parents. Like parents, students learn best in an environment that values, supports, and nurtures their abilities.

Erin Gruwell's class in room 203 in a high school in Long Beach is a good example of students recognizing their value. Most people wrote Erin's students off as losers, gang members, or worse. No one expected their attendance at school, but her insistence on accepting them as they were, and her methods of reaching them through journals and story writing, not only kept them coming to school, but as their website states:

> We have created this website because we want to form a community like the one we formed in Room 203, where people feel safe, accepted, and understood. We hope that The Freedom Writers Diary will inspire you to succeed academically, change your community, and share your own story. (www. freedomwritersfoundation.org)

Students in the ACT (Academy of Communication and Technology) program at Chico High School show up for another reason. They learn their English, math, and social studies by interacting with the subject matter and representing it through technology. Visual poetry, Shakespeare on video, and Washington politics set to music make for amazing learning. Kids show up early and stay late.

Attendance is not a problem when kids are valued, connected to teachers and learning, and they find the curriculum meaningful. Your attendance data will tell you whether value, connection, and meaning — all feeling tones — are taking place at your school.

Behavior Counts

Behavior in your school also starts with our first step, attitude. My first visit to St. Hope School gave me an idea about behavior and attitude. I arrived on the campus after winding through the streets of inner city Sacramento to find the school tucked into the corner of a dead end street. The field behind the school's fence looked like a cross between a self-proclaimed motocross arena and a landfill.

As I toured the school with the principal, Herinder Pegany, the kids explained why they were there. All the children I met stuck out their hands, introduced themselves, and then said, "I'm going to go to college."

It didn't mater what grade level. Kindergarteners shook my hand and said, "Hi, I'm Suzy and I'm going to go to college."

Later as I met their parents for a workshop, they had the same statements, "Our kids are going to college."

That attitude brooks little nonsense for bad behavior. It isn't necessary. Attention is gained from working toward the goal of college, not toward goofing off, acting out, or being a gang member. What is valued is working toward college. What is not valued, nor given attention, disappears.

Behavior has to do with norms. Look at the norms in your school. Determine what is valued. Your collaborative says reading is of value. Recognize and value the readers and the parents who support those values. Valuing and supporting what you want is a great deal more effective than fighting against what you don't want. What you resist persists. Put your effort into recognizing what you want.

Grades and Assessments

Quarterly grades will give you another picture of what kind of progress you're making toward your goal. One collaborative choose K-2 reading. Yours may be similar, or it may be math or science you wish to see improved. You may choose to concentrate on reading for a few years. As you see success, you may choose to move your focus to math. The choice will be up to your collaborative. Grades can give you an idea of how long to stick with your choice.

If you've been in education any length of time, you know grades are relative. As much as we try to make them objective, it's not possible to compare one teacher's grades with those of another teacher, or one school to another.

Let me give an example. I visited two schools located twenty miles apart. The first school was in an affluent area. Parents were CEOs of companies and made large donations to the school. I attended their science fair one year and felt like I was in a NASA space station. On my visitation day, my goal was to spend time in their special education resource program. When I walked in, the children were discussing dangling participles and split infinitives. I walked back outside to check the door to make sure I was in the special education class. I was. This was not a typical discussion for children with Individualized Education Plans.

The next day I visited the second school. This one was on a Marine Base with enlisted parents' children. Because students moved in and out before the year was over, the transiency rate for the school was higher than their average daily enrollment. I visited their special education resource class and found eighth graders struggling over second grade reading material and sixth graders having difficulty adding double-digits numbers. The room was full. The teacher told me these were the children having the most difficulty. If they used the usual special education criteria, they could have qualified 90 percent of the school.

There is no way to compare grading systems between the two schools. I'm sure third graders received *A*'s and *B*'s in both schools. The children earned the grades based on what they accomplished, taking their situations and abilities into consideration. Grades will give you some feedback about how well things are going, but they may not give you the full picture.

State test results are going to give you a better picture of progress, but these tests take time to show changes. It's easy to give up if you don't see major change in results the first year. Or even worse, if you do see a change and it's a drop! Improvement occurs when you make a systemic change and maintain it over time. That's exactly what you're doing when you undertake the A-G steps in P-TAG. I repeat: systemic changes take time.

Progress Leads to Success

The length of time involved means we need to highlight our progress toward the change. Short term results like the number of additional books in the library, will show the parents and staff that change is occurring. The long-term results, such as children being able to read at grade level, may take a year or more to show up. It's easy to be discouraged when something doesn't look like it's happening right away. That's why we identify several actions to take under each goal, collect data to show progress, and communicate the information as often and in as many ways as possible. Waiting a year for test results may be something teachers are used to doing, but parents want to see that in all kindergarten classrooms, 95 percent of the families read fifty pages a week this month. Actually, teachers may be used to waiting for test results, but they sure like to hear that too!

You are changing a culture. You are breaking down the silos and inviting other to participate in learning. You are building skills, and you are building trust. That takes time. Allow it to develop. Watch the results. Live Oak Unified did. St. Hope Charter did. Sun Empire Elementary did. They are seeing the results in their state test scores. Check the appendix to see some of their results. There are more schools like these. Your school and your collaborative can do it too.

Even More

We could stop here and say that's good. Your collaborative has succeeded. Test scores increased. Or you might conclude attendance is up, behavioral referrals are down, and test scores have improved. So it's good, but there's more. Sounds a bit like one of those ads on TV. Buy this for $15.95, but wait there's more. There is more and in this case, it's not as easy as the ad on TV.

The more is not the quantifiable stuff that goes into a data chart or on a line graph. It's part of that evaluation of feeling. Let me describe some of the more difficult to quantify aspects of what happens when you've created an opportunity for families to become involved in learning. You'll note I'm going even farther back than our collaborative's goal. I'm going back to the purpose behind the collaborative, which was to engage families in school and learning.

Attitudes change. Family engagement in schools means the attitude in the school changes. Walk around your school a year after you've begun your collaboration work. Contrast the feelings that were prevalent before you began the work and where you are now. You'll feel the difference. The classrooms have a different atmosphere. There are different people in the rooms. The children behave differently. Acceptance may not be on a chart on the wall, but it's in the faces of those in the hallways and in the classrooms. Ask your teachers, parents, and the students. The Las Vegas school noted earlier buzzed with energy and excitement. I was only in the building for a couple of hours and I felt the energy. Your school will feel different when attitudes have changed.

Skill levels will increase. Previously unengaged parents are showing up and sharing how much fun math games are, how their children are reading more and with better comprehension, or how their own reading has improved. The mom who thought she couldn't help her child in school is tutoring other children in math. Teachers feel more confident showing parents what they're teaching, and finding ways for parents to reinforce activities at home.

Nikki Lleneras, a parent collaborative first grade teacher in Live Oak Unified, told me she had taken a short medical leave. The day she came back, the children in her classroom were asking for their parent activities. The substitutes were great, they told her, but they didn't know how to send things home for their parents to do with them. Now that she was back, they wanted activities their parents could do with them at home.

The children's comments lead to an unquantifiable result — bonding. I'm not even sure if bonding is the correct term to use, but the kids know what it feels like and how to describe it. A loss of closeness and energy occurs among family members when parents and children sit in front of a TV screen night after night. Playing a game, reading together, doing an experiment, or making cookies brings about conversation and companionship. A bond develops around the things you do because you enjoy them, talk about them, and interact over them. There's interest and support.

Dynamics Change

We don't always realize the impact we have on children. We are models, and children imitate models — whether good or not so good.

After working in schools for so many years, I can usually pick out which parent goes with which child. Occasionally, I can tell by the physical resemblance, but most often, I see similar mannerisms and interests. I was waiting for a plane recently and watched a man exit the ramp. He had on blue jeans, a western shirt, a prominent belt-buckle, a well-worn cowboy hat, and boots. My first guess was that here was a rodeo cowboy. He looked very comfortable being who he was. Right behind him was a boy of about six wearing jeans, a western shirt, a cowboy hat, and boots.

He had yet to earn the belt buckle, but I felt sure he would. Just like Dad.

When parents and children share common interests, a special bond develops. Children watch what parents do. They are interested in the same things their parents are, and want to do things with them. When learning is important to the parents, it is also important to the children.

Learning, talking about learning, and being a part of learning becomes comfortable. My family reads. We had bookcases full of books in every room. We went to the library every week. It's what we did. Reading was important to us as parents, and we modeled that for our children. They are still readers today, and will set the same example for their children.

Community Support

The other by-product of family engagement is community support. Parents who are pleased with their schools and whose children are doing well become big supporters of the school. Those very same parents may be plumbers, electricians, doctors, or lawyers. They may sit on corporation boards, be members of Rotary or Elks, and talk across the back fence to neighbors. Community members are often related. You may find the firefighter who comes to talk to the kindergarten knows about your school from his brother, the police officer knows about the school from her sister, and your mail delivery person has grandchildren at the school.

Community support is no small matter. Hamilton High School's

Ray Odom found visiting the homes of incoming freshman paid off when he requested a bond issue to build a library. The local elementary school was asking for a bond measure for classrooms at the same time. Voters signed Ray's petitions with ease and they overwhelmingly approved the library. The elementary school stalled at the signature stage. Ray had promised that the library would be open two evenings a week for community use, and he kept his word.

Ray's efforts hit the media. There were a couple of articles in newspapers and a TV interview, but the small bit of publicity he received would never have been enough to overcome obstacles if there had been any. Ray overcame any obstacles long before he ever made the request for the bond support. His interest in the community, his commitment to his students, and his efforts at making his school the best possible ensured the bond passing.

Satisfaction

The final piece that defies measurement — another state of feeling — is the satisfaction that comes from what happens for kids and families. Financial reward is not usually the driving measure for a teacher or school administrator. It's not in promotions or teacher of the year awards. Those things are nice, but the real reward for most of us is watching children learn a new concept. Their eyes light up and we know they "got it."

Parents feel the same way when their baby smiles for the first time, says his or her first word, or takes a first step. Parents sometimes lose the thrill when school starts because they no longer believe they are the primary teachers. Bringing parents back into to the learning process allows them to continue to enjoy the act of discovery. Teachers and parents teaming up with learning helps create an environment where every child can succeed.

Dr. Joni says...

√   But wait, there is more!

√   Evaluation includes the head and the heart.

√   Progress counts toward success.

Chapter VIII

F — Follow-Through

Although it is Step F in the A-G system, the letter does not stand for failing grade, but for "Follow-Through." Step F keeps the system on target for success. A major factor in the credibility of any collaborative is reliability in follow-through. The initial enthusiasm for the plan must be evident in day-to-day delivery. It's so easy to say you'll give a call, talk about something later, or fix the faucet. Make sure you're clear about who's going to call, talk, or fix the faucet before you leave the meeting and establish a timeline for completion. Putting this in writing helps build accountability, and can be used to document tasks completed.

This is not a *got-cha* step. Without follow-through, there are no results. After a meeting, send a written reminder of those things agreed upon and persons responsible for completing tasks. You can create further accountability by asking team members for updates at each meeting and offering assistance if they need it in completing responsibilities.

Follow-through is an Action Step

Healthy eating results in more energy, and a sense of being in control. Even if my head gives me every rational reason why this is right for me to do, it still takes effort to follow through and do the work to make it happen. I've read several motivational books about health and healthy eating. I also went to a workshop that taught alternatives for healthier eating and the attendees decided to help each other follow through by offering online support. I then visualized myself in the healthy state I desired. I needed to think and act in positive ways to bring about what I wanted. In other words, I followed my plan by putting myself in situations where I could bring about a healthier body.

There are ways to assist your collaborative with follow-through. Each plan contains a variety of incentives. You build incentives for success while you develop both the team and the plan. Some of the intrinsic incentives include the reasons you want to do your project, your vision board, and the mission statement. In your mind, you see where you want to go and you direct your energy into getting there.

Extrinsically, the goals and activities you lay out for your school will produce the desired results both in and out of the classroom. Your checkpoints are the goals and objectives you set up in your plan. If your goal is to fix the drinking fountain, then your objectives may be finding a person and the financial resources to fix it, scheduling a time for the work to be done, and checking for completion. There are many objectives and it's easy to determine if a step is completed — yes or no.

In our example, Lincoln School, the goal was for every student completing the second grade regular education program to read at or above grade level. Their objectives were more specific. By the end of the school year, all kindergarten children should know the names of and the sounds made by the letters of the alphabet, recognize one hundred sight words, and have listened to fifty books. Lincoln School developed a system of checking for progress toward these objectives throughout the year.

Kindergarten teachers usually have a checklist of alphabet letters for each child to see if the children know their letters. Parents, now included in the plan, will be checking at home as well. Oops, Suzy doesn't know Q yet. Teachers and parents need to share a duck's quack quick. Juan is having trouble remembering the letter Z. A trip to the zoo to see a zebra isn't an affordable field trip for the school, but might be for a parent. Zebra's in zoos are definitely in books and on the Internet. There are many ways for teachers and parents to provide more opportunities to learn Z. Teachers and parents sharing the activities they're using for learning Q or Z makes it easier to reinforce what Suzy and Juan are learning.

You can see that the follow-through for a more complex learning project is more complicated, but the results are as recognizable as whether the drinking fountain is fixed. Do all the children know their letters by the end of kindergarten — yes or no? The answer needs to be yes.

It's time to revisit, revitalize, and revise those follow-through drivers so you realize the vision you set out as you began the process. Your P-TAG team must break your learning goal into specific objectives that lead to the goal. Then the team must develop and follow-through on action steps to achieve the objectives and the final goal. The evaluation is simple — it's a question of "yes" or "no." Either you achieved the objectives or you didn't. If the objectives were not finished, you need to determine a different plan of action.

Follow-Through Requires a Positive Attitude

The major factor for your success is attitude. Attitude is a mind-set, a way of thinking, a point of view, or an opinion. Attitude is everything. There's a whole chapter about it earlier, but attitude bears reviewing when it comes to following through with your P-TAG plan. If you are a leader in this plan, others will want to know if the plan is going on a shelf or if this is actually going to happen. They'll watch you for that clue.

Attitude starts before you roll out of bed in the morning. Your head starts going before you even open your eyes. If your first thoughts are, *Oh no, another day at school. Why can't it be Saturday? I hate that place. I hate working there. I hate the people there. Nothing ever goes right;* then you can bet the objectives for implementing learning activities will not be a top priority. Looking through want ads would be a more productive objective.

Wake up to thinking about the possibilities and opportunities at your school. Consider capacity in the shower. Ponder potential over coffee. Deliberate decisions while driving to work. These activities are fun, creative, and full of positive energy. The smile is real. It shows the genuine passion you have for your work and your teammates. Your attitude says let's go for it. Let's do it every minute of everyday we're here. Let's make learning happen. The learning objectives your team set will be high on your list of activities for your day.

Remember the movie *Yours, Mine and Ours?* Attitude is about yours, mine and ours. People around you notice your attitude. If you're upbeat and positive about an idea, it's easier for others to be upbeat. They catch your positive energy. It's also more difficult for others to be negative in light of your enthusiasm. When you express your enthusiasm for parents visiting your school, others will notice. When you demonstrate your acceptance of parents in your collaborative, others will follow suit. When you model learning activities for parents and children, others will do the same.

Remember Your Vision

One of the best ways to stay focused on your goal and follow it through is to remember your vision. You created a vision board and vision statement for exactly those times when you were ready to throw in the towel. When you toured your school before starting your P-TAG work, you had a vision for what you wanted your school to be. You imagined what it would be like in a school when staff, parents, and students fully engage. Your vision for your school included teachers collaborating for the benefit of all students; parents involved in workshops, assisting in classrooms, and working with their children at home; children talking about things they'd learned in class and from their parents the night before. You saw the school running smoothly and imagined the front page of the newspaper reporting your great test scores. Remember that vision? Remember those feelings? Think about them now. Close your eyes and walk through your ideal school in your mind.

Got the picture? Good. That's what you need to see and feel everyday. That is the feeling that will carry you through on days when the drinking fountain cracks again, a father calls to complain about his son's grades, or the budget hits an all time low. Take a deep breath and remind yourself that what you want is the ideal vision you hold in your mind. You're going there. The water fountain is only a minor issue. It's fixable. The phone call will end well. As long as you have money in the budget for coffee, you can still meet with your parents. If there isn't money, Grandpa Joe or Suzie Jones will bring some. There will be more fountains, parent issues, and budget crises, but your goal is for an engaged school where learning is happening and morale is high, and you must follow through to reach your goals.

I recommend placing your vision board in a central location. It is also important to create a vision statement that is easy to remember. For the visual people at your school, the vision board reminds them of their ideal. For the auditory folks, hearing the vision statement brings a picture to mind of what they want the school to look like. If you have a daily public announcement time, include the vision statement, or an abbreviated form of it, as a sign-off tag line. That's what Lovettsville Elementary, in Loudoun County, Virginia did. Morning announcements always included, "And remember...Lovettsville Elementary is 'the school that begins with love.' " That short tag line represented the vision and every parent, student, and staff member could (and would) finish the phrase, "the school that..." However you do it, use visual and auditory reminders to follow through with your vision.

Follow-through begins early in your first project. It's going on while you work on the water faucets. Follow-through includes calling those who haven't been showing up. Drop by to see them. There may be a problem to consider, such as the need for childcare in order to attend a meeting. Or maybe parents don't always understand the conversations if English is not their first language. Follow-through is addressing the collaborative member's needs to help them participate and share what they have to offer.

Extra Benefits of Good Follow-Through

One of the outcomes for collaborative members, as well as those affected by your projects, is that participants gain new skills and insights. I don't take a class or seminar to rehash information I already have. I want new ideas, new ways of looking at things, and new results.

If I join a weight control program, I want to learn new strategies for eating healthier. If I go to all their meetings, and follow their advice, I want to see the scale go down. I also want to pick healthier foods and have more energy. There are expectations about what I get out of putting my time and energy into a new adventure. Your collaborative members have similar expectations. Learning needs to occur. The goal may be for student learning, but activities will cease if adults aren't also learning and growing.

Look at the number of new learning programs we've had in education over the years. "New math" developed not because the old math wasn't working for children, but because it gave adults a new set of learning tools and ways to approach math. "Whole language" was another approach for adults to test out learning theory. The children accepted whatever approach we used. As educators, we look for new learning techniques to make it easier and better for children to learn, but also to test our skills at learning new methods and reenergizing our teaching skills.

Parents are learning too. Some may be learning skills for the first time while others are dusting off skills they haven't used in many years. All learners need to feel like they are gaining and growing. They need to value what they are learning. They need to put their skills to practical use. In other words, they need to see the fountains fixed and students reading.

Follow up with both teachers and parents. Ask what they are learning. Find out what skills they are gaining. Ask directly and individually. Make sure participants are building their skill base. An occasional survey assessment is helpful. For those participants who may be reluctant to share their opinions, a survey allows them an opportunity to let you know if you're on track or not.

Progress

Assessing the progress of your plan is a major component of follow-through. A walk through your school hallways tells you if the drinking fountains are working or not. Your walk is part of the follow-through. You're checking to see if the team's objectives are being met. Thank the custodian for keeping the fountains working. Call a member or two of the group that made suggestions for fixing the drinking fountains. Tell them you value their input. Each one of these actions is a form of follow-through.

Your reading collaborative project can take a similar approach. One of the objectives for the first and second grade students was for each of them to read fifty books. An activity was to do silent reading twenty minutes a day. Sit in K-2 classrooms during reading time. Visit classrooms during the reading time. Don't forget to bring your book. When the students see you reading they know it is important to you. Tell them about the great book you're reading. Be sure to take time to congratulate the teacher and the students on how well they are doing with their reading. Invite collaborative members to drop by with their books during reading time so they can enjoy the same experience.

Follow-through is necessary. We all have plans that ended up on a shelf collecting dust. Those plans did not include follow-through. Without follow-through, the staff members will feel this is not a high priority and parents will be reluctant to give time to the project.

Follow through with Activities

Your collaborative, whatever its goals, will have activities or events to move their project toward completion. These activities could take the form of a school-wide work weekend to fix the faucets, a series of workshops to demonstrate reading, a book fair, parent reading nights, or a "be-a-reader" overnight campout at the school. There are multitudes of activities possible for school collaboratives.

Project events need to be scheduled, supported, and publicized, which is another part of follow-through. Identify who's responsible to make sure these events are scheduled and they don't conflict with something else like the Little League playoff game or the church carnival. Events need lead time to get students, teachers, parents, and community members enthusiastic and participating. Your collaborative needs cheerleaders and publicists. The more the word goes out, the better your event turnout.

You also need cheerleaders and publicists for ongoing activities, such as your in-school daily reading or the at-home reading time. You can easily forget these activities without regular reinforcement. Keep the momentum through newsletter articles, teachers' notes home, and progress charts posted in central areas of the school.

The town I live in adopted the book, *Three Cups of Tea, One Man's Mission to Promote Peace…One School at a Time.* by Greg Mortenson (2006), as its book of the year. There were book studies, "Teas," and presentations based on the book for months. That's not all. The author came to the Chico State University Campus to give a talk. Over two thousand people attended. It was front-page news. There weren't too many folks in town unaware of the book. That's cheerleading and publicizing in a big way and it pays off. You want your collaborative's goal for reading to be as successful.

Follow-through Means Training for Success

The plan your collaborative designs may require training. It is entirely possible your first or a subsequent collaborative will pick a project that needs more specialization. Let's say you're in your third year of working with collaborative groups within your school. This P-TAG group has chosen math as an area to work on. They want to work with algebra, which is part of eighth grade curriculum, but algebraic thinking is actually introduced in the earlier grades.

This collaborative's goals include creating K-8 math experiences which promote math skills. It's a great goal and certainly one to help with student performance and ability level. For the third grade teacher who hasn't done anything with algebra since college twenty-seven years ago, this could be a challenge. For the mom whose math utilization is balancing the checkbook and figuring out the grocery budget, dealing with algebraic formulae can be quite a stretch.

There may be someone on staff or at the district level to do workshops to build or refresh teacher and parent math skills. You may need an outside resource. Your prior work of building that welcoming and accepting environment, making your school accessible, and building on strengths, is now going to pay off. Parents are now likely to feel more comfortable about not knowing how to do something. Teachers are more likely to admit this isn't their strength. All are more willing to work together to learn new skills. This is the time to embrace new learning together with that ideal school vision in mind.

Training may require outside help and even the expenditure of some funds. Funds are easier to acquire when you have a specific goal, community support, and a record of increasing student performance. You may find funds in your budget earmarked for math skill development, have a grant writer on your team, or there may be someone in your collaborative with great math skills. When you look in other places to meet needs, you'll find exactly what you require.

How are the Kids Doing?

Speaking of follow-through — we all track student performance. Administrators are acutely aware of test results. Teachers want to know how their class did. Parents want to know how their children fared. All want to know how the school ranked on the state tests. A P-TAG school will be especially interested in standardized scores, because they have become much more aware of student performance. If parents are spending time and energy at home reading or working on math activities with a goal of improving their children's learning, they're going to look at grades and test results.

Tiger Woods is an excellent example of a family putting energy into a child's early learning with big results. And, where I live, the Lohse family was into baseball. They had a baseball diamond in their backyard. They supported all their kids' baseball teams from Little League up. One of their boys made All League each year he played for Hamilton High School. Kyle Lohse recently signed a forty-one million dollar extension to his contract with the Cardinals. That's performance — backed by parental support of their child.

Another set of high performers I've met are five-time Grand National Fiddle Champions, Tristan & Tashina Clarridge. The two were home-schooled by their mom and spent many hours a day practicing with their fiddles. When you hear them play, you know all that practice paid off.

Follow-through is energy expended over the long run. Not all families put as much energy into a sports or music career as the Woods, Lohses, or Clarridges. But energy is energy. When families spend time reading, reading improves. When they spend time playing math games, math improves. When they try out experiments in the kitchen, garage, or garden, Einsteins are born.

When a family puts energy into their child's activities, not sporadically, but regularly, the benefits are evident. Ten minutes a day can make a huge difference in a child's performance on any subject. Twenty minutes a day can change a life.

Dr. Joni says…

√ Follow-through is an action step.

√ Expended energy always produces results.

√ Twenty minutes a day can change a life.

Chapter IX

G — Go For Great!

Your school is good now. You have the data. You know how you're doing. You're pleased so far. Your school is good, but you want to leave a great school legacy.

Administrators, teachers, and parents want to know they made a difference. Along the way, they'd like to feel satisfaction and joy in a job well done. They want to review and relive the achievements they've made. In schools, most of those achievements rest on the success of the children and the families you serve. Is this the year your good school becomes a great school? You can make this the best school year ever!

A school is average when a number of its students succeed. A school is good when most of its students succeed. And a great school? Well, that's when *all* of the students are successful learners.

When administrators, teachers, parents, and students have a "we can learn" attitude, they will. When a school has an attitude that says, "We can succeed," they will. When a school knows they're great, they are. Attitude is about knowing you can do anything you want. Attitude helps move a school from good to great.

Today is the first day of that best school year. Start today. Talk to families. Identify who will be on your collaborative team to move your school forward. Schedule a meeting. Tell your staff and parents you endorse a P-TAG system, and together, make it work for your school.

You're on your way! You are ready to "Go for Great!"

The Goal: Success for All

We could stop with the examples of Tiger Woods, Kyle Lohse, or the Clarridge fiddlers and let all of those successes seep into our pores in understanding the difference families make to their children's successes, but there's more. I'm back to sounding like the TV ad, but there *is* more.

Individual performances are certainly wonderful. Kyle's pitching helped the Hamilton High School baseball team, but he didn't pitch every game, and he needed eight other players to back him up in case someone did make contact with one of his fastballs. Every school wants individuals to achieve to their highest potential. If you look at mission statements for one hundred school districts, I'll bet ninety of them mention something like "each individual reaching his or her highest potential." It's what schools are all about.

The ideal vision is to have every child reach his or her highest and best. It is wonderful when one student reaches stardom, but we want all students to soar. St. Hope wants all of their students to go to college. Every parent wants their child to be successful in whatever way they evaluate success. Goals must be about more than a few children gaining recognition.

Success is defined by whatever you perceive it to be. If you define it as children earning *A*'s in every subject, then most schools will earn a good rating. There are many schools where children earn high grades. If you define success as children reaching proficiency or above on the state tests, then you'll find most schools working hard to reach that goal. There are some schools, however, where students haven't earned the top grades or haven't quite topped out of proficiency, but they are still great schools.

Let's revisit Hamilton High School. In their first run for distinguished recognition, there was a question about their eligibility. It seems they had rave reviews, but their test scores weren't as high as other recommended schools. A team from the County Office of Education visited to determine if they were worthy of the recognition. I was a member of the team.

We visited classrooms and talked to staff members who had nothing but wonderful things to say. At noon, we met with about thirty students, freshman through seniors. Our staff escort left us with this admonition: Ask anything you wish. The students will tell you if the school is truly deserving of the recognition or not.

We asked the students to tell us about their school. Then we asked, "What do you like best? What do you like least? Why should we recommend you? What makes this school so great? Many of you are transfer students, why do you come here?"

The students weren't shy. They were candid about their school. They felt their school was the safest place in a community with a reputation for gangs, crime, and poverty. Kids transferred into this school because they and their parents perceived it to be excellent. The students said the teachers cared about who they were, what they did, and whether or not they showed up. Every student in the room was adamant — they deserved to be a Distinguished School.

When the interview was over, I found Ray Odom in his office. While I was telling him about the students' comments, I noticed he kept looking out the window. Finally, he said, "Sorry, I'm keeping an eye out for my truck. I loaned it to one of the students a couple of months ago because his broke down and he needed transportation to go to work. I'm expecting him to bring it back today."

Administrative job descriptions don't contain clauses that say visit the home of every incoming freshman or loan students your truck when theirs breaks down. It also doesn't include contacting baseball scouts, but Ray does all of the above. It's no wonder the students feel safe and cared about when they attend school there. Hamilton High School earned the Distinguished School Award that year, and two more awards since then. They also had the highest rate of students going to college in the county.

When you "Go for Great," excellence is your target. You defined excellence when you toured your school and created the vision for your school. Your collaborative defined excellence when they created a vision statement. Your school and families defined excellence when they caught the vision and wanted their children to go to your school. We want to be a part of this. Open your doors and welcome the parents who are ready and willing to help. Build your collaborative, create your plan, follow through, and reap the benefits for and with your administrators, teachers, parents, community, and, most of all, your students.

What you do with the P-TAG concepts presented in this book is up to you. You and your P-TAG collaborative determine your vision. You and your P-TAG determine your goals. You and your P-TAG determine your greatness as you move your school from a good school to a great one and eventually to a school of excellence — a place where every child succeeds.

Dr. Joni says…

- √ It's up to you.
- √ You are on your way; you are going for great.
- √ Today is the first day of your best school year ever.

Chapter X

Engaging Parents When Funds Are Fizzling

I recently attended a conference of school administrators and the only topics were budget, money, shortfall, cuts, and layoffs. It's hard to watch everyone struggle. This chapter is intended to show you how connecting with parents does not require large amounts of money from your budget. You can start with the cost of a pot of coffee. It takes that little and the results are huge. So please sit back, relax, and see how you can add tremendous support to your school on less than the cost of a cup of coffee.

Education has a reputation for under funding, but some years are worse than limiting book purchases or canceling a workshop after school. Deep cuts may feel like trying to breathe underwater after the air tanks ran out five minutes ago. You are wondering if selling perfume at Macy's isn't a better way to make a living. Anything would be better for an educator than facing a group of students whose learning you can't support.

Details of budget shortfalls vary. The particulars of how or why don't matter. You know what it is like to be in the midst of a deficit.

You cut bus routes. You cut librarians, music teachers, and art classes. You hire part-time custodians and pray they show up. Each of us has our own story about how money shortages played out in our schools. This is familiar territory for those of us who have been in education for more than three years. Perhaps this downturn looks worse than what you've been through for many years, but you've dealt with this boom/bust economic situation before. This time, make it different. You can use the situation to your advantage. If you have lemons, make lemonade, lemon meringue pie, and lemon bars along the way.

School Finance 101

Education finances are complex. School district budgets are a lot like doing the itemized investment deductions on your tax forms. You can deduct this item if it's less than one thousand dollars and you didn't spend the money on the third Tuesday in March in a city that begins with *S*. Check the tax laws to see if they've changed before you submit. Most of us go to a tax consultant or do a short form. We're willing to pay whatever the cost so we won't have to deal with all the intricacy.

School boards hire business specialists to take care of all the budget details. The business director follows the laws and tells us not to spend a thousand dollars for the new faucet out of special education funds. We can spend the money out of deferred maintenance if we have bathroom improvements in our five-year plan. His or her advice is valuable to keep us out of trouble with the quagmire of categorical funding guidelines, but we want to be in charge of where we put the money to support school programs. We want to comply with laws.

Special education money goes to special education programs, but we also want the capability to envision what we want and need to do for students, and to invest the money we receive in the best ways to make that vision a reality. Compliance demands, budget constraints, and student needs are a delicate balance.

Budget Shortfalls and Cuts

School district revenue comes from a variety of sources. Federal funds become available to schools to provide an array of programs. The biggest federal money sources these days are Title I funds for No Child Left Behind (NCLB) and special education funds through the Individuals with Disability Act (IDEA). These funds are significant. They make up 7 to 10 percent of a state's education budget with most funds going directly to school districts. Even more significant than the dollars are the mandates the funds carry with them. To receive funds under NCLB, there are requirements for districts to utilize specific learning standards, test performance, and accountability to prescribed policies. Under IDEA, all identified special education children must have an Individualized Education Plan and receive services as outlined in their plan. The income from the government is supposed to match the outgo for programs, services, and support for identified students at the school level.

State funding and/or local taxes make up the bulk of the remainder of school income. These funds also come with mandates usually prescribed in law, further defined in education code, and even further delineated in local district policies. Other sources of budget funds come from grants, fundraisers, donations, or other ingenious ways we've figured out to bring in the extra revenue for the video camera or a second computer for the eighth grade class.

Staff salaries account for approximately 80 percent of school budget expenditures. School districts hire administrators, teachers, aides, bus drivers, cafeteria workers, noon-duty supervisors, custodians, and coaches. If there are adequate funds, they then hire librarians, art teachers, and music teachers. Any remaining funds go into supporting these folks in teaching and taking care of children as well as keeping up the facilities in which they work. It's simple and yet complex. Many decisions are made around who teaches what curriculum, and how much support goes to teach each subject. Mandated curriculum drives a good deal of what we are required to teach. NCLB test requirements call for all children to be proficient in reading and math by 2014. College entrance requirements usually mean four years of high school English classes. Schools base funding decisions on the perception of what it takes to support teaching to mandates.

Discretionary funds are those dollars we can put aside in the budget for the projects we want to complete. Sometimes those projects include fixing the leaky pipes in the boy's bathroom or making the parking lot handicap accessible. The project might appear discretionary because there's no money anywhere else in the budget to complete it, but law requires school safety and handicap accessibility. Fun projects, like purchasing the technology teacher a video camera so the kids can film the school play, are only considered in a school year with a more luxurious income. We look to good years of funding to provide the items we can't squeeze out during a tight budget year.

From Tight to Slash and Burn Budgets

Tight budget is the technical term for "can't get any more out of this turnip." We've allocated all the money available for salaries and support and there isn't more anywhere. We've all experienced tight budgets. There is no money for the video camera and duct tape is holding the pipes together in the boy's bathroom for now. We gave up on the camera and the bathroom isn't aesthetically pleasing, but it is safe, it works, and it's on the list for fixing as soon as funds are available. In those years, we just stay alive and survive.

Slash and burn budgets are another story. The administrator who is already using duct tape on the bathroom pipes is now looking to find, from funds already allocated for salaries, ways to cut more from the budget. We're now at staff cuts. We've no choice but to let people go from their jobs. If there are any librarians, art teachers or music teachers left, they should be concerned. Aides, bus drivers, and cafeteria workers are looking over their shoulders. Teachers with only a year or so of teaching are worried about a pink slip and those who have been around awhile may be wondering how they are going to work without an aide and how many children will be in their classroom. We are down to basics, and in these rough economic times, as NCLB puts it, we're below basic.

Remember Your Dream

This may sound like the time to return to your thoughts of Macy's or Wal-Mart, but I'd like you to consider another option. Go back to the dream you had for your school when you said yes and signed the contract to work there. You saw something in the kids there. You saw a direction for the school. There may be no funds right now, but look at what you'd like it to be anyway. Create the dream. Go back to the vision you created when you toured your school at the beginning of the P-TAG process. Picture in your mind what you'd like your school to be, and you will discover ways to make it a reality. Dwelling on what currently is, will only get you more of what currently is. Dwelling on the budget shortfall will only get you more budget shortfall.

The Kids are Still Coming

Open your eyes. Look around. The kids are still coming to school. They are still excited. They still want to learn to read. They still want to show you their math tests or the story they wrote. They're curious about why the guinea pig squeaks or whether the seeds they planted will come up. They still show up every day. They haven't seen the budget. They don't believe the economy is in trouble. They're in your classrooms, and it's still your job to help them learn. Make them a big part of your dream. See their future. Now see yourself making a difference for them.

There's no denying the economy is in trouble, but tight budget times give us an opportunity to find other ways to make things happen. Can't get oil for gasoline? We'll develop hybrids. No money for a movie? We'll rent a DVD or better yet play a game or read a book at home. It's time to find alternative ways of dealing with the loss of funds.

It's easy to find a target to blame — blame the economy, blame the feds, blame the mandates, blame legislators, or blame board members. Blaming may relieve stress, but it doesn't solve the problems. Spend the next ten minutes blaming whoever and whatever you'd like and then let's agree to drop it.

What You Want Your School to Be

Instead of faultfinding, use your time to revamp your thinking. Look at what you have and how you can use it to your advantage. There are students. There are teachers. Yes, there may be fewer than before, but there are teachers. There are cafeteria workers, bus drivers, custodians, and some aides. There are parents. There are... Please stop and go back a sentence. There are parents.

Parents, hmm, yes, those folks with the same interests we have — their children.

For years, educators have had the luxury of teaching children in a school setting. As educators, we've been fortunate enough to go to college, learn subject matter, and learn how to teach. We went into schools with the idea that teaching is what we do. It's what we do, not what someone else does or can do. Teaching is who we are. We don't often consider someone else might help or like to teach as well.

Educators do their jobs fine — except in places where English is a second language, where there's poverty, or where parents in a household work long hours and don't spend time with their kids, and so forth. You can name the situations where we have trouble serving. You see these situations in your schools and talk about them in the teachers' lounge. You may have marginally considered the value of parents, those adults — mom or dad, grandparent, foster parents or others — who take care of children, but do you want to ask for their help?

It may take something like a drastic drop in the economy to get our attention to change our thinking. If that's what it takes, let's use it for the benefits it can provide. The downturn gives us the opportunity to get to know the parents — the people who can help children learn the very things we are trying to teach. And the benefits of engaged parents will continue even when economic times are better.

Economic hard times mean a change in thinking, a change in action, and a change in how we support learning. We often change out of economic necessity. I've heard it said, "Necessity is the mother of invention." Changing our thinking doesn't require money. Changing our thinking doesn't require a line item in the budget. Changing our thinking doesn't need approval from the business manager.

Parent Engagement

So go back to the group that has a similar interest to what we do in schools — the parents. They may not have taken education courses nor done an internship on early childhood learning, but these are the folks who are most interested in the outcome of their children. Also, because of the economy, families may only have one parent working, may have more time on their hands, and may need a focus where they feel like they are making a difference or contributing somewhere. Parents have time and energy right now. We need people to help children learn. We're all in this economic situation together so let's channel and use what we have to our advantage.

The Obstacles

There are only two obstacles to including parents in their children's learning. One obstacle belongs to educators and one to parents. The obstacle we educators need to address is not what you may think. It's not socio-economic status, education level, or ethnicity. The obstacle is perception. It's our mindset — our thinking about the way it is, and the way it's always been. Parents have always sent their children to school. Teachers have always been the instructors. Parents don't know how. Parents aren't interested. Parents don't want to help. Parents…

These are perceptions and live only in what we think we know. The second obstacle is also a perception. This mind-set lies in the thinking of parents. I have four children and a doctorate in education. You'd think I'd know what to do when it comes to supporting my children's learning, but like any other parent, I got lost in the system's mind-set early on.

My first offspring to go to school were twin boys. They had different teachers. Christopher was in a class geared toward pre-kindergarten while James was in a kindergarten class. Their teachers used different curricula and each teacher had a different set of goals she wanted for the children in her class. I was working more than fifty hours a week and I depended on their dad to do school work. If I had extra time, I spent it coaching T-ball, a fun and enjoyable way to spend time with my kids.

It didn't take long for me to realize I didn't know what my children were learning at school. I knew how to find out, but was uncomfortable asking questions and wanting help. Therefore, I didn't know how to support my children's learning, and I didn't have any warm fuzzy feelings about showing up at school or doing more at home. It became easier to let the teachers do it and I would do what I had time for and felt like doing at home.

Parents don't often have the same background I do in education, but in my experience working with numerous groups of parents, they express the same feelings of disengagement and ambivalence about trying to get involved at school. Unless someone — an administrator, teacher, or other personnel — is there to encourage, provide direction, and ask how it's going, nothing will change. Teachers will continue to teach. Parents will continue to coach T-ball and kids will learn what they can from both their teachers and parents. It would be more effective if we were on the same page.

Economics of Parent Engagement

Because of the economic and budget situation, you will be trying to determine what sort of impact engaging parents will have on your budget before you're willing to commit yourself. Initial parent engagement takes little of your budget. Coffee klatches one morning a week are a great place to start. All you need is a coffee pot and coffee. It doesn't even have to be Starbucks. Spend a bit of time with parents talking and sharing over a little early morning start-up juice. Answer a few questions, share a program or two, and listen to parents share. Soon they will feel welcome, comfortable being at school, and may want to know what they can do to help.

Perhaps they'll want more and you'll want to put some funds

into childcare or translators for a workshop. Even then, some parents are willing to do childcare or translation as long as someone else does it next time. Again, little money is required.

Your teachers can create materials and do workshops to demonstrate parent engagement activities, or you may decide to hire consultants, such as Family Friendly Schools, to support you with an ongoing and measurable program of family engagement.

Willingness is the Key

It doesn't take a lot of money to engage families in learning. It takes your willingness to involve them. The benefits are worth it. Parent engagement will allow you to provide learning support on whatever budget you have available. From a cup of coffee with parents in your office, to Live Oak's workshop nights, to Murphy's Family Resource Centers, the choice is yours, but the benefits for engaging your parents include:

- Improved test scores

- Increased attendance

- Reduction in behavioral referrals

- Improved community awareness and support

- Increased levels of self-esteem for parents and children

Schools that are using P-TAG concepts are showing increases in these areas. My own research and that of others bear out these results. The appendix includes data from schools using family engagement strategies. Engagement works. It has worked for these schools and it will work for your school.

The budget is at crisis point. There is little doubt it is affecting all of us, but crisis is often a catalyst. This is your opportunity to uncover a well-kept secret — some of the most important talent you have available to you — the parents in your school.

Dr. Joni says...

√   What is doesn't have to be.

√   The kids are still coming to school.

√   Parents are waiting to help — engage them and prepare for success!

Appendix Contents

- Parent-Teacher A to G (P-TAG) Process Checklist
- Research Results - Live Oak United School District, CA
- Research Results - Sun Empire, Kerman Unified School District, CA
- Research Results - St. Hope Charter, Sacramento Unified School District, CA
- Welcome to Parent Playbooks
- Sample Pages from the Parent Playbooks

Parent-Teacher A to G (P-TAG) Process Check-List

School Name_____ Date_____

A-G	Description/Comments	Ad	Te	St	SS	Pa	Ot
Attitude	School staff and parent attitudes about your school and their, child's learning, and their willingness to be engaged; Welcoming environment						
Building Engagement	School staff and parent relationships; people getting to know each other; Two way communication						
Collaboration	P-TAG collaboratives of school staff and parents established to create relationships, build trust, and solve an immediate need at the school: Degree of Engagement						
Develop a Learning Plan	P-TAG collaborative ready to engage in learning with children at home; Support for Home Learning						
Evaluation	Check in to see how school staff and parents are doing in both relationships and learning for children						
Follow-Through	Double checking to make sure staff and parents are engaged; following up with those who need additional support						
Good to Great	Greatness is ALL groups-staff, parents, children, and community are engaged in learning						
Sample							
Attitude	Welcome signs are out; office staff trained for guests and phone calls; working on teacher's lounge atmosphere; parents aren't yet involved with school or learning	H	M	M	H	L	DK
Your School							
Attitude							
Building Engagement							
Collaboration							
Developing a Learning Plan							
Evaluation							
Follow-Through							
Good to Great							

Key: H-high M-medium L-low DK-don't know (dk also means it's time to go find out)
Highly recommended: Do a quick check list monthly and watch your progress grow!!

Live Oak Unified School District, California

LOUSD Growth in English/ELA 2003-2008

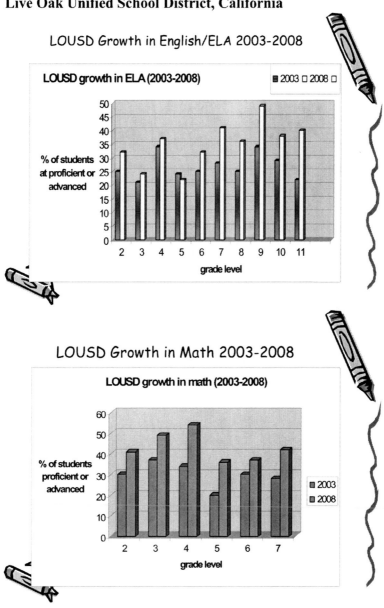

LOUSD growth in ELA (2003-2008)   ▣ 2003 ▢ 2008 ▢

% of students at proficient or advanced

grade level

LOUSD Growth in Math 2003-2008

LOUSD growth in math (2003-2008)

% of students proficient or advanced

▣ 2003
▣ 2008

grade level

Sun Empire, Kerman Unified School District, California
St. Hope Charter, Sacramento Unified School District, California

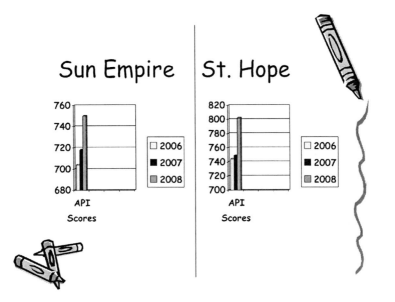

Welcome to Parent Playbooks

My goal in writing the Parent Playbooks was to involve parents with their childrens' education. I wanted to provide exciting activities related to the grade-level curriculum. Each activity is fun and easy for parent and child while being matched to a specific national or state learning standard.

Sample activities from the Parent Playbook series are included in the next few pages of this book. As you look over the samples, you will see the grade level in the square under the activity title. Each activity includes number of people, time, and materials required, followed by a description, a notation of the standard addressed, and a place for parent notes or variations on the activity.

Many school districts are using the Parent Playbooks to engage parents in their children's education. My greatest joy is when I receive feedback from parents, students, and school personnel that the Playbooks are making a difference in the lives of families.

If you are using them, I would love to hear from you.

--Dr. Joni

For more information or to order Parent Playbooks, email info@familyfriendlyschools.com, or phone 1-800-890-7794.

Alphabet Hunt

Number of People: 1+ **Time:** 10-20 mins

Materials: Small sticky notes

Description

Using 26 sticky notes, write one letter of the alphabet on each paper. Randomly stick the letters on objects in the living room (but don't hide them). Now, while you're fixing dinner, give your child one letter name at a time and tell him to go find it.

Variations: Rather than give a letter name, you can give the sound of the letter. With a more experienced reader you can give a word and have the child find the letter that begins that word.

Time Challenge: Time your child each time you play the game. Challenge the child to beat his previous time.

Essential Standard Derived from Nat'l and State Standards

English Language Arts Standards: Reading
Distinguish letters from words.

Notes for This Activity at Your House

Donated by: Linda Armstrong   Taylors, SC

Find It on the Map

Number of People: 2 **Time:** 15 mins

Materials: World map, United States map

Description

Put a world map and a map of the United States on the wall in the dining room. At breakfast time, do some map investigation. Ask your child to find the United States, California, and some of the other states around California. Have them find the seven continents and the four oceans. Which map is better?

Essential Standard Derived from Nat'l and State Standards

History - Social Studies Standards
Locate on maps and globes their local community, the state, the United States, the seven continents, and the four oceans

Notes for This Activity at Your House

Math on Wheels

Number of People: 2+   **Time:** 20 mins

Materials: License Plates

Description

While traveling, select a license plate. Using the digits on the plate, write down as many ways as you can to create a particular number. For example, if the license number is TGY 4631, how many ways can you create 6?

There is one 6 on the plate, but 4 + 3 - 1 also equals 6. (4 + 6) - (3 + 1) = 6. You get the picture. How many more can you find? Now change the number to 8.

Essential Standard Derived from Nat'l and State Standards

Math Standard
  Simplify numerical expression using the order of operations with grade-appropriate operations on number sets.

Notes for This Activity at Your House

Clean Up Your Pennies

Number of People: 2   **Time:** 30 mins

Materials: Jar, 1/4 c. vinegar, pinch of salt, 15 copper pennies, iron nail, scouring powder

Description

Have your child clean an iron nail with scouring powder and set it aside. Let him put vinegar in a jar with a pinch of salt. Add copper pennies to the mixture. Let them sit for a few minutes. Then have him drop the clean nail into the mixture with the pennies. Talk about what happened. Do either of you know why? Look up copper acetate on the Internet in case you don't know.

Essential Standard Derived from Nat'l and State Standards

Science Standard

Chemical reactions are processes in which atoms are rearranged into different combinations of molecules.

Notes for This Activity at Your House

REFERENCES

Bartlett, Sam, Vie Herlocker. *Building Better Schools by Engaging Support Staff.* Galax, VA: ENGAGE! Press, 2007.

Brown, Michael. *The Presence Process: A Healing Journey into Present Moment Awareness.* New York, NY: Beaufort Books, 2005.

Constantino, Steven. *101 Ways to Create Real Family Engagement.* Galax, VA: ENGAGE! Press, 2008.

Constantino, Steven. *Engaging All Families.* Lanham, MD: Scarecrow Education, 2003.

Duch, Barbara. "*University of Delaware: Problem-Based Learning.*" http://www.udel.edu/pbl/

Epstein, Joyce. "Issues and Insights." In NNPS: *A Research Based approach to School, Family, and Community Partnerships, Type 2,* Issue No. 19, Fall, 2005.

The Freedom Writers. "The True Story." www.freedomwritersfoundation.org/site/c.kqIXL2PFJtH/ b.2286937/k.5487/About_Freedom_Writers.htm (Accessed July, 2009).

Henderson, Anne T, Karen L. Mapp. *A New Wave of Evidence: The Impact of School, Family and Community Connections of Student Achievement.* Austin, TX: Southwest Education Development Laboratory, 2002.

Henderson, Anne T. Testimony for NCLB reauthorization. Here's the website: http://www.ncpie.org/docs/Henderson.Testimony.

Senate.March2007.pdf

Mortenson, Greg, David Oliver Relin. *Three Cups of Tea: One Man's Mission to Promote Peace…One School at a Time*. New York, NY:Peguin Book, 2006.

Samples, Joni. Parent Playbook: *Activities for Kindergarten to Second Grade*. Orland, CA: EdSuccess, 2005.

Samples, Joni. Parent Playbook: *Activities for Preschool*. EdSuccess. Orland, CA: EdSuccess, 2007.

Samples, Joni. Parent Playbook: *Activities for Sixth to Eighth Grade*. Orland, CA: EdSuccess, 2006.

Samples, Joni. Parent Playbook: *Activities for Third to Fifth Grade*. Orland, CA: EdSuccess, 2004.

Scott, Elizabeth. *"Understanding and Using the Law of Attraction in Your Life."* http://stress.about.com/od/lowstresslifestyle/ss/happy_2.htm (Accessed July, 2009).

ADDITIONAL RESOURCES

Building Successful Partnerships: Guide for Developing Parent and Family Involvement Programs. Bloomington, IN: National PTA, National Education Service, 2000.

Canfield, Jack, Mark Victor Hansen. *Chicken Soup for the Soul* series. Deerfield, FL: Heath Communications, 1993.

Covey, Stephen. *The Leader in Me*. New York, NY: Free Press, 2008

Collins, Jim. *Good to Great, Good to Great: Why Some Companies Make the Leap... and Others Don't*. New York, NY: Harper Collins, 2001.

Delisle, Robert. *How to Use Problem-Based Learning in the Classroom*. Alexandria, VA: ASCD, 1997.

Henderson, Anne T., Karen L. Mapp, Vivian R. Johnson, and Don Davies, *Beyond the Bake Sale: The Essential Guide to Family-School Partnership*. New York, NY: The New Press, 2007.

Marzano, Robert, Debra Pickering, and Jane Pollock. *Classroom Instruction that Works, research-Based Strategies for Increasing Student Achievement*. Alexandria, VA: ASCD, 2001.

Payne, Ruby. *A Framework for Understanding Poverty*. Highlands, TX: aha Process, Inc., 2001.

Payne, Ruby. *Understanding Learning the How, the Why, the What*. Highlands, TX: aha Process, Inc., 2001.

Reeves, Douglas. *20-Minute Learning Connection*. New York, NY: Simon and Schuster, 2001.

Ruiz, Don Miguel. *The Four Agreements: A Practical Guide to Personal Freedom*. San Rafael, CA: Amber-Allen Publishing, 1997.

Samples, Joni. *Taking the Guesswork out of School Success: A Standards Approach*. Lanham,MD:ScarecrowEducation, 2004.

About the Author

 Dr. Joni Samples is a popular keynote speaker and trainer in the area of family engagement, and is the Chief Academic Officer of Family Friendly Schools.

Her background combines academic credentials with practical service as a lifelong educator. She has served as a superintendent of schools, special education administrator, curriculum and instruction director, CEO for early childhood programs, coordinator of career and technical programs, and a teacher for regular and special education, as well as teaching at the university level.

In her third book, *The Parent Connection: An Educator's Guide to Family Engagement*, Dr. Joni shares her Parent-Teacher A-G (P-TAG) system for helping schools engage parents in the education of their children. Her experiences as an administrator, teacher, and parent allow her to blend theory and practice. Her suggestions are research based, but practical, and will provide a foundation for home and school engagement.

Dr. Joni's interest in parent involvement began with her four children — twin sons James and Christopher, and daughters Jennifer and Carolyn. The kids provided daily learning insights that she translated into a weekly newspaper column. An article about learning fractions came from measuring ingredients to make muffins with Christopher. James' science fair project about rat reproduction resulted in several articles on how to develop a scientific hypothesis and test it out, as well as what to do with rats that have become too numerous to keep in one cage, house in an entire garage, and are threatening to take over the household!

The popularity of the newspaper column led to Dr. Joni's first book, *Taking the Guesswork out of School Success: A Standards Approach*. This book stresses the importance of parent engagement in a child's learning, and shows schools and parents how they can help each other.

Dr. Joni's *Parent Playbooks*, a three-book set, followed. The *Playbooks* present home-based activities matched to national learning standards at the different grade levels.

Dr. Joni is a past president of the California County Superintendents' Education Services Association. She currently serves on the board of the Family Area Network (FAN), California Department of Education; is a member of the Alliance for School, Family, and Community Partnerships; and is on the planning team for California Action Plan for Partnerships' Parental and Community Involvement.

CPSIA information can be obtained at www.ICGtesting.com

232764LV00003B/1/P